THE NEXT LEVEL

THE NEXT LEVEL OF ADVENTURES

A SIMPLE GUIDE TO HELP YOU IMPROVE YOUR MOTORCYCLE TRAVEL SKILLS AND MAKE THE ADVENTURES YOU HAVE ALWAYS DREAMED OF

PAVLIN ZHELEV

COPYRIGHT © 2019 PAVLIN ZHELEV

The texts featured in this book belong to the author and they are protected by the Copyright Law and other such related rights.

THE NEXT LEVEL OF ADVENTURES

A simple guide to improving your motorcycle travel style

and making the adventures you have always dreamed of.

ISBN: 9781798626832 Paperback

This book is dedicated to the adventure rider community. They completely changed my mind and the way I view the world. Their stories about unknown places and outstanding people from across the globe have opened my eyes and pushed me to become a real motorcycle traveler. I strongly believe that collectively, we have the power to change the world and make it a much better place!

CONTENTS

WHAT TO EXPECT FROM THIS BOOK 9

PART ONE: UPGRADE YOUR KNOWLEDGE

1. HOW TO GET STARTED WITH LONG ADVENTURE TRIPS?......................10
2. 5 THINGS THAT YOU NEED TO KNOW BEFORE YOU GO......................13
3. HOW TO PLAN A BETTER TRIP..14
4. HOW TO MAKE IT CHEAP?...20
5. HOW TO GO AROUND THE WORLD WITHOUT ROBBING A BANK?.........24
6. THE SECRETS NOBODY EVER TELLS YOU..27
7. HOW TO TRAVEL AND STAY ALIVE?...30
8. WHAT I LEARNED FROM MY TRIPS?..34
9. WHAT ARE YOU DOING WRONG?..37
10. 5 THINGS THAT I WISH I KNEW WHEN I STARTED...............................41
11. HOW TO STAY MOTIVATED ON LONG TRIPS?......................................44
12. HOW TO MAKE FRIENDS EVERYWHERE AROUND THE WORLD?............47
13. TIPS TO AVOID MOTORCYCLE ACCIDENTS..51
14. HOW TO GET MAXIMUM FUEL EFFICIENCY?.......................................55
15. FERRIES, VISAS, TEMPORARY IMPORT AND CARNET DE PASSAGE.....58
16. HOW TO RIDE A MOTORCYCLE IN A FOREIGN COUNTRY?...................62
17. HOW TO MAKE THE RIGHT DECISIONS?..65
18. TIPS FOR SOLO RIDERS..70
19. TIPS FOR GROUP RIDING...73

PART TWO: WHAT YOU REALLY NEED?

20. THE DEFINITION OF THE BEST ADVENTURE MOTORCYCLE..................76
21. ABS OR NOT – WHICH IS BEST?..81
22. SPOKE WHEELS OR ALLOY WHEELS?..83
23. HOW MUCH GEAR DO YOU ACTUALLY NEED?....................................86
24. THE BEST LUGGAGE SYSTEM..89
25. READ THIS BEFORE YOU START BUYING...92
26. MOTORCYCLE SAFETY GEAR...94
27. BUY PROPER MOTORCYCLE BOOTS..97
28. HOW TO FILM YOUR ADVENTURES?...99
29. HOW AND WHERE TO STORE YOUR ADVENTURE VIDEO FILES?.........101
30. DO I NEED A TANK BAG?..103
31. WHAT I HAVE IN MY MOTORCYCLE SADDLE BAG?............................104

PART THREE: GET READY FOR REAL ADVENTURES

32. OFF-ROAD MODIFICATIONS..106
33. MOTORCYCLE TRIPS IN THE WINTER..109
34. HIGH ALTITUDE..113
35. WHAT TO EAT AND WHAT TO AVOID?..115
36. HOW TO STAY HYDRATED?...118

WHAT TO EXPECT FROM THIS BOOK?

Firstly, I would like to sincerely thank you for buying this book! This help is highly appreciated, and all the profit will be reinvested in my future trips and of course my Youtube channel. As I have always said;

'The world is going to be a much better place if we help, instead of hate each other!'

I hope that you already have my first book 'How to become a better long distance motorcycle rider', because it is actually like the first necessary step that you have to take before the real jump into the next level of becoming an a real motorcycle traveler. If you haven't, I strongly recommend that you read it. Otherwise, it would be extremely difficult to accept some of the tips and the tactics that I am going to share with you. You can purchase it from my website: www.rtw-adventures.com or from Amazon.

In the next pages, I will do my best to help you with everything you don't know, or you are still not sure about. I have only one simple requirement, one condition! To open your mind and see the world with the eyes of an adventurer! To forget about everything you know, or what you have heard from the mass media, and be ready to face the real world. To meet real people, to listen to real stories! They are not always exciting and fancy, like in the Hollywood movies, but they will help you to realize that we are all the same, and above all else, they are REAL.

I will also try to convince you that the most important part of any trip is not the bike, not the gear, not the trip itself, and not even you! The most important part of any trip is the people. The wonderful men, women, and children that you are going to meet while you travel.

Of course, I will share some very practical tips and hacks with you to make your trips much easier than they are right now. With just a few words, you will discover the next level of adventure on your bike!

What you are not going to find here are riding techniques. I don't consider myself to be a riding expert or some kind of adventure legend. I am an ordinary man, just like you and 99% of the riders I have met in the last couple of years. Yes, I know how to ride a motorcycle, and I have done a large number of trips around the world, but to know how to ride, and how to teach people to do it are two very different things.

You will also discover that I am a bit of a minimalist, and I try to keep as few things as possible with me; However, it doesn't mean that you have to be the same. Everybody is different, and each of you will have and develop different preferences. Do whatever you think is right for you and your riding style. The idea behind this book is to show you one approach, a different way to see the whole picture, not to teach or change the habits that you already have.

With that being said, let's jump on to the next level….

How to get started with long adventure trips?

All right, if you have come to this point, it is obvious that you are already a motorcycle traveler or at least you have some trips already under your belt. Perhaps you want to take things a step further and start your first real adventure trip, but you are not sure about it yet. There are many small things, important details, and questions to consider at this point. With just a few words, you are not 100% convinced that you are ready…and now what?

So…firstly, I am here to tell you that this feeling is absolutely normal, and we have all had it when we first started out. In the following chapter, I will give you some very practical advice about how to gain the confidence you need to take the next steps.

Listen closely. Do not pressure yourself, and do not let anybody control your decisions. Pieces of advice like, "you will learn on the way, it's nothing scary" are maybe right, but it really depends on the person. For example, (as you know I love examples):

For a new rider, with two months riding experience, this will be very dangerous advice. On the other hand, for someone who has ridden bikes for 30 years, but who has never been on an adventure trip, this will be absolutely fine.

What I am basically trying to say, is that you have to build up confidence; and the problem is, just like with anything else, it cannot be done for just a month or two. It's the same as when you start visiting the local fitness center, and after just two months, you then go on to enter a Mr. Olympia competition. You can do it, but I can tell you right now before you even go there what the result will be. It will be the same when you start anything new in your life - learn to ride, to drive a car, to swim, run or whatever. You will need a certain amount of time to learn the basic skills.

The best way to gain some confidence is to make it on different stages, or as we call it "Step by step."

Number one is to learn how to ride and how to control your bike. By this, I mean the actual bike that you are going to use on the trip. Yes, it sounds easy, but many riders never try their bikes off-road. For example, you might say – yes, but it's not necessary, I only plan road trips. I will agree, you don't need to become an off-road expert, but at least you need to know how your bike reacts on such terrain. Also, once you have that experience of riding off-road, riding on the asphalt will be like a piece of cake.

Of course, the best option will be to take some off-road courses with a certified instructor; but as I said, even the simple back or gravel roads will give you some idea what is about. On long trips, you never know what you are going to face. Even if you plan only road sections, you still might hit some construction works, a flooded river, a destroyed bridge or something similar. Having these basic off-road riding skills will help you in those moments.

What brand or model of motorcycle to take depends on your personal preferences and the trips you are going to make. Remember, it is just a tool, the travel is what really matters. In my previous book, I have written a full chapter on how to choose the right motorcycle.

After you have completed the first step, (learn how to ride your bike), you can start with some simple day trips. It is very important to test your bike with the luggage in place. Especially if you are planing to use hard cases as they will significantly change the weight distribution and the way you feel on the bike. Load up your entire luggage and go on a simple one-day ride. Spend at least a couple of hours on the road, just to have an idea of what is about.

The next step will be to extend it a bit, maybe two-three days with a camping option. This will give you an idea of what you really need and what is useless, because it will be about the same on the longer trips. Don't make the same mistake that most of the new riders make and take too much luggage. In the last couple of years, I have talked a lot about the weight and how important is to travel as lightly as possible. If you still don't get it, I will advise to read my first book again, or take time out to watch some of my YouTube videos on that topic.

You have to understand that what I, or someone else will say, it doesn't matter because at the end of the day, you are the only person who needs to deal with all of the circumstances that come from the decisions you take.

Now, we are coming to a more serious and difficult part, a one week trip. Plan the route carefully. The first trip needs to be something easy for you. Such as a destination that you already know. Load the bike, as lightly as possible, set your GPS or paper map, and then go! I will suggest the accommodation to be a mix, some camping, and some hotels. This exercise will teach you how to plan the time more efficiently, how to navigate yourself, what constant speed works for you, and much more. Also, it will help you to reduce the luggage even more than you already did. Another significant benefit from the trip is going to be that you will have an idea of what to expect, where and what to eat. You will also know how much it will cost you. All of this will be the best preparation for your long trip.

After that one week trip, you might find out that it is not what you were expecting and decide to do something else instead. This is exactly what happened with a friend of mine. He was very motivated, bought a bike, all the gear, (most of it useless if you ask me); but anyway, he went on his first long trip, from Germany to Bulgaria and that was it. He is even still trying to sell the bike now because he is moving to another country. So, it is not unusual for this to happen, and these short trips will save you a lot of time and money if this is going to be the case.

When you complete these first three steps, at a guess, it will take you at least six months; then, you will be ready to move to the last and final step, and go on a long motorcycle trip.

First, you have to ask your wife, mother, father, girlfriend or whatever relation you have. Believe me, this will be the most difficult part of the whole trip. I know that many of you will play macho and will say that it will be what they say, but you know what I mean. I have a video about it, it's a bit old, and the audio is not good, but the information there is priceless, go and find it on my channel. The title is 'How to get permission for a long motorcycle trip?'

The second and another very important decision will be, how are you going to travel? Alone or in a group? There are many discussions on this topic, but only you are the person who knows the answer. Do not listen to what your friends will say, only you will go on that trip, and you know yourself much better than anyone else does.

After all of this is done, you just need to find some free time; which is not easy by the way! You will need money, a destination, and of course, some documents, then you are ready to go.

The night before the actual day you are due to start your trip, you will be a bit nervous. In fact, I would bet that you won't be able to sleep at all. There will be so many questions:

Is this the right time?

Am I ready, have I made a mistake?

What about if something goes wrong?

Am I able to compete it alone?

There will be many more, but all of these will disappear once you start the engine. Then, you need only to concentrate on the important stuff, and the silly things will be left far behind…

Now, I am going to give you some very simple advice, and I really hope that you will follow it.

- The first one is to keep everything as simple as possible. Trust me on this.

- Less is always better. More luggage, gear, accessories, electronics, and gadgets will almost certainly equal more problems.

- The weight always matters. Even the most skilled riders will confirm this.

- A constant speed is better than a top speed. Remember, the most important thing is to come back home safe and in one piece. It is not a race and no one will count the time.

- Always believe in people's goodwill. We are all the same.

*****

5 things that you need to know before you go

Okay, there are of course many more, but I think that these five will be enough for you to get the idea. They worked very well for me, and I cannot see any reason they won't work for you as well. My advice will be to read it carefully. Don't just follow the rows and go to the next chapter. You have to let them into your mind, and they need to become like second nature, like an unconditional reflex, or to say it simply the way you think it.

1. **The bike is like a woman.**

   - Respect it
   - Ride it
   - Take care of it

If you break any of these rules, you will be punished.

If you don't respect the power of your bike and the way the bike reacts in different situations or terrains, guess what? You will be punished really badly, and you might even die.

Don't ride it often - it will fall apart, dead battery, flat tires, rust everywhere...I guess that you have seen some abandoned cars or motorcycles in your neighborhood.

Without care – well, even the most reliable models will give up at some stage.

Exactly like women, no difference! I apologize to the female readers, but it was said with an educational purpose in mind.

2. **There will be some bad days.**

Rain, cold, snow, ice or all together at the same time. Once you accept that fact, everything is going to be ok. Please do not say that you are ready for that – no, you are not, but you will be next time once it has happened. We cannot fight with nature, and we don't have to. Trust your common sense and pray that the gear will do the job properly.

3. **Safety is just an illusion.**

Yes, correct, safety is just an illusion. You have heard the phrase:

   'Ride safe.'

Even I say this all the time. Everybody rides safe, and no one ever wishes to have an accident, but sometimes, shit just happens. All of the safety gadgets or gear you might have cannot protect you if your luck disappears for a moment. Once you swallow this, everything is going to be much easier.

4. **Better planning equals a better trip.**

Yes my friend, a better plan is equal to a better trip. Some will say that the real adventure begins when the trip is going wrong. Agreed, but don't even worry about it, the trip never goes exactly as you planned anyway. There will be many changes and possible adventures, and you don't need to look for it. They will find you!

5. **Better to travel alone than in the wrong company.**

You will learn this one way or another. The more you travel, the better you will understand what I wanted to tell you. Yes, to travel alone has some cons, but it is the same for everything in our lives – there will be always pros and cons, the important part is to find the right balance!

I should have told you:

You will miss family … I am sorry, but I cannot help with this!

*****

How to plan a better trip?

So now, after a number of successful trips under the belt, you are still unsure that you are doing things absolutely right. You have a feeling that you may miss something; perhaps something big and you cannot understand what it is. If everything I just said is not aligned with your thoughts, great, you can skip this chapter and move on. But if I hit the jackpot, keep reading, and I promise that you will find what you are looking for.

Alright, so how do you plan a motorcycle trip? Actually, there is nothing that is majorly difficult with it. As I always said, I respect the riders who travel without any plans, but I prefer to be ready.

'Everything you do before the trip will help you during the trip!'

I keep saying that because it is so important. Do your homework, find as much information about the countries you plan to visit as you possibly can. The time will be very well spent once you get there. With that being said, let's get to the tips:

1. Free time.

It is obvious that without free time you cannot go anywhere, why do I even say that? Because my friend, the free time you have will tell you where you can go. For example, if you live in Western Europe and have only two weeks holiday, it will be impossible to ride to Mongolia and back. You can, but you will have to ship the bike. If you plan to ride it, then you will not have enough time. It is around 15,000km in total. When you divide it into 14 days, it's more than a 1,000km per day. Some people might say:

If I travel with 200km/h, I need 5 hours, and I need to stop 3 times to fill the tank and one cigarette...maybe less than 8 hours to make 1,000km...

I think that if you have the same ideas about your trip, then you are about to learn just how wrong you are.

Yes, in Europe, on the highways, it is easy to achieve 1,000km per day, definitely not for 8 hours, but easy to do it. However, when you go to countries like Russia, it will be very difficult to attain that goal day after day. When you get into some bad roads or even dirt roads, it will be hard to make even 300km per day.

Plan the trip carefully and do not punish yourself. The number of km per day you can achieve will depend on the roads, the bike, and your riding style. Do not plan more than you can handle. It is always better to plan less and ride more, than the opposite way round.

The example I can give you was from my trip to Mongolia:

The Russian visas we had were valid only for 30 days. This is the maximum you can get from the embassy. While 30 days may sound like a lot of time, the problem is that Russia is so big. From Kiev (Ukraine) to Ulan Ude (Russia), this is actually the last big town before you enter Mongolia, and we had ridden almost 6,500km. We did it in 8 days, no actually, we had one day off in Novosibirsk, which meant that we did it in 7 days. So if you divide 6,500km by 7 days, it's more than 900 km per day. Again, many will say this is not a problem, I can make it.

Don't even say it or think it before you do your research. That's why the preparation is so important!

There are no highways there. Actually, it is one road, with a lot of construction works and traffic. Yes, we did it, but it cost us more than 14 hours, some days 16 per day, strict riding and a lot of ass pain. Anyway, we spent about a week in Mongolia, and we still needed to ride to Russia to get out. When you see the whole picture, you realize just how tight the time we had actually was. On that trip, I did almost 18,000km in just 35 days. This was actually more than 500km per day. This is something I will never do again unless I really have to. Do not be like me, think twice, or even hundreds of times before you even start, because, after that, it is going to be too late.

2. The right destination.

Where do you really want to go? What part of the world do you want to see the most? What terrains you are ready to ride? Do not try to imitate some famous riders or their routes. You are a unique person, you have your own preferences, and you can make your unique trips!

What is good for one doesn't mean that it will be good for you as well! Everybody is different! The example I can give you now is from Pamir Highway in Tajikistan. I was there, and I loved it. In fact, this was the best place I have ever been so far, but a friend of mine did it last year, and he said:

'Well there is nothing so interesting there, just bad roads, dust, muddy rivers, and bad hotels, I will never do it again!'

I hear the same now after my trip to Pakistan, India, Nepal, and Bangladesh. Many people have asked me:

'Why the hell do you want to ride in these terrible countries? There are so many far better places around the world? Why?'

Because I love challenges! I love it when someone says: 'You cannot do it!' It motivates me and actually gives me the power I need to prove the opposite.

I like to step out of my comfort zone and to test my limits. To see what can I do. How much further can I go in order to reach the next level of adventures?

The result, was that I enjoyed every single minute of the trip and I will always do it again with pleasure!

So…it really depends on the point of view. Choose the places _you_ want to visit!

3. Do not book in advance.

Well again, it really depends on the trip. For example, with some destinations like Genua or some other busy seaports in Europe you really need to book your ferry in advance. However, in most cases, it is not going to be necessary and could be useless, because with a motorcycle, you never know when and where you will finish the day. There are so many possible obstacles; bad weather, mechanical or health problems, unexpected traffic, closed roads or borders…

You might also see a really nice place or meet some great people and decide to stay a day longer. Who knows? You might fall in love and want to spend more time with that person or even completely change your life. Be flexible, and try not to lock your trip too tightly with bookings. Hotels, hostels, or a room to rent can be found almost everywhere around the world. In the worse case, you can always take your tent.

4. Paper maps.

Again, about the paper map – I really love them, don't you agree? When I plan my trips, I always make the route on the map. There are 3 very good reasons to do this:

- First, is to see where I have to ride and to try to remember it, just in case I lose it. Before and during the trip you will check the map so many times, that without even wanting to or trying, you will remember it, or at least the most important points on it.
- The second is to be able to calculate the km and hours per day. You can do it before the trip or during the trip. What I usually do is put some sticky notes on the specific sections of the map, just to have an idea what to expect later when I get there. I also draw some symbols like a tent for overnight, cross for a church, a question mark for something curious or any other mark to check out while I ride. This will help you much more than you can even imagine.
- The third is to see what is around and what else I can visit while I am there. All of this information will help you to make some changes and plan your route more efficiently. A paper map also gives you the chance to talk with the locals and to receive some really nice recommendations or routes.

There are a couple of things you have to keep in mind: The paper map might have first been produced a long time ago. Almost everybody on the planet knows how to read it, or at least will be able to point you where you are in any case that you get lost. They don't need power or the internet. With a minimum effort, you can have the maximum efficiency if you just learn how to use it. Last but not least, they cost almost nothing compared to the rest of the expenses you going to have.

5. Money – how much will it cost you?

It really depends on your personal preferences. You can make it very cheap or travel like an Arabian Sheikh. For exactly the same trip, with exactly the same bikes, and the same number of days, two people could spend totally different amounts. How much it will cost will always depend on you. Determine a budget, add some unexpected costs, and try to stay on budget. There will be some pluses and some minuses, but if you are strict, the total amount will roughly stay the same. For example, if your hotel budget is 50 euro per day, you can always book a better hotel and sleep in cheaper accommodation or even in the tent when you have the chance to do so. In the end, you will keep to the budgeted amount without calculating every cent.

6. Plan days off.

This is so important! Plan at least one day off per week. Otherwise, you will be so exhausted, and you will not entirely enjoy the trip. In some nice and interesting cities, one day is not going to be enough. For example, in Central Asia, the famous places like Bukhara, Samarkand (Uzbekistan) or now in Delhi (India) were so interesting, there were so many things to see that I stayed a lot longer than I could have ever thought possible. You have to plan all f these carefully, or you will miss a lot.

From my own experience, I know that it is much better to plan more days off and skip it later than the other way around. In the end, we travel for pleasure, and it is not going to be that way if you have to ride 1,000km per day. Do not play this game, because you will regret it, and it doesn't matter what bike you have.

Also, by planning the days off in advance, you will be able to see the weak spots of the plan and change it before you go. It is much better to skip some points or places and have more time for another. You actually never know in advance what you are going to like and what you will not. You might think that a specific town will be great, or this section you will enjoy it much more than another, but as I said, you cannot be sure unless you have been there before. With a few words, plan less km and more days off.

7. Pack the right gear.

Again, do your research before the trip. Do not take the things you might or never use. For example, you are not going to need your warm under layers or many clothes in Africa because it will be hot. However, you definitely will when you ride into the north. Rain gear is not necessary in the desert, but it is very important in Ireland for example. The same with everything, jacket, pants, a tent and many more.

Another example I can give you now is from Pakistan. My riding friend, Anif, got a light mesh jacket, which was good around Karachi, Lahore, and all the busy roads, but once we started to climb the mountains, he was freezing. So actually, I needed to give him my switcher for a couple of days just to be able to complete the trip.

It was the same with his riding gloves; he had only a thin summer set. On the other hand, I knew what temperatures I would face there, and I had the proper gear for every scenario. Simple research before the trip will help you to make the right choices. All of this will also help you to reduce the weight by taking only the necessary things, and as you already know, weight always matters!

8. Chose the proper bike.

For long highway trips a big, powerful, and heavy bike is going to be great; but on bad or dirt roads it will be a big challenge. We all know that, but when the trip is mixed, highways and dirt roads, what is the right thing to do?

I will suggest, or at least, this is what I would do, is to choose and prepare the bike for the hardest part of the trip. For example, if you have a 10,000km trip, but 1,000km are bad or dirt roads, choose and prepare the bike for these tougher 1,000km. It is okay to ride 9,000km nice roads with a light bike, but it will be very hard to have a big and heavy adventure motorcycle for 1,000 km spent on bad or dirt roads.

As you already know, I love examples, so on my last trip to India, I was riding Royal Enfield Himalayan. It is a local Indian bike with only 25 horsepower and a total weight of 180kg. It is obvious that this is not a bike for highways, but I also know that the highways in India are not like the highways in Europe.

In some of the sections, like the one from Delhi to Srinagar, I faced such bad traffic and not so good roads, that I actually spent the entire day filtering between trucks cars, people; and riding in dust, gravel, sand, mud, and everything you can imagine in order to complete the trip. This was the easiest part. A week later, I had to ride the Rohtang pass in terrible weather conditions, and I was so happy that I had a light bike with me.

Another important factor to consider is that in the case of breakdown, you need to find someone to fix your bike, and this will be an impossible task if you don't have the right motorcycle.

At the end of the trip, I made my conclusion that the Royal Enfield Himalayan is not the best adventure bike on the planet, but it was maybe the best bike for me to explore India and Nepal.

So my friend, always make sure that you have the proper motorcycle for the destination you going to travel to and across.

9. Backup options.

Always be ready with some backup options. For example, if the route is going to some mountainous areas, but the weather might change, be ready with an alternative route and still continue your trip. Another example is to rent a local bike if yours breaks down. Or maybe even consider visiting another country, because your visa has expired. To work a couple of days, if you run out of money, or use your credit instead of a debit card and of course many more choices like this.

Even if you never need it, the backup options will give you peace of mind and help you to feel much better. This is how our brain works - no exceptions!

10. Sort your things at home.

Family, relations, kids, friends, and your job. Do it before you go. Do not even think that you can handle it from a distance! It will be very difficult, almost impossible, and definitely will ruin your trip.

*****

How to make it cheap?

I have received a lot of questions about how I can afford to travel so much. Well… I cannot teach you how to travel without any money, but in this chapter, I will give you 10 tips to make your trip as cheap as possible.

Many people, including some experienced riders will advise you that it's an expensive hobby and you need to be a rich man to afford it. Okay, but as you know, I never fully agree with anything before I really test it. For me to travel with a motorcycle is not actually that expensive, as long as you follow some simple rules.

In fact, if you ask 10 people the same question:

'How much does it cost to travel with a motorcycle?'

You will probably receive 10 different answers, but what is interesting, is that they will all be right. How is that even possible? As usual, I will try to explain with more details or at least inform you more about what it is that I do.

The price of the trip depends on the destination and also on your personal preferences. In this chapter, I won't discuss exactly the cost of the trip, because I have already talked about it in my first book. However, what I will do, is to give you 10 very practical tips on how to travel cheaply.

N: 1 – Buy an affordable motorcycle.

I said affordable, not exactly cheap because I still believe that the truth is somewhere between the words, 'too expensive' and 'super cheap'. Okay, but here someone might say:

'The topic is how to travel cheaply, the price of the motorcycle itself it doesn't matter!'

Let me explain why to you with a few more details:

- When you have an expensive bike, you will definitely have expensive gear. For example, hard cases, tank bag, windscreen, better seat, tires, spare parts, and many more. For new models, all of that stuff is majorly overpriced.

Again, many may resist and say that this is a one-time investment, but it is not. Nothing lasts forever, and the gear needs to be changed very often, especially if you travel a lot.

- The maintenance of that bike will be double the price. In many cases, you will need a proper garage to do it in, and they charge about 100$ per hour. With most of the new bikes, you cannot do anything without a computer and special software.

This is a proven fact. It doesn't matter what anyone says, I have seen this with my own eyes many times before.

- Most of the new and expensive motorcycles will only use premium petrol, which is usually about 10% more expensive.

Also, this could lead you to some unexpected problems during the trip. For example, if you filled some bad petrol and the engine refuses to start. This problem happens very often with the new motorbikes, and of course, it will cost you a lot of money to resolve it.

- From a security point of view, in many places around the world, you will need a garage or paid parking. You cannot just leave it on the street, even if you have a disc lock, a big chain or even alarm system. Nothing is 100% secure! The more luxurious the bike, the better protection you will need.

- Because of the fancy bike you have, many of the prices will be higher for you.

You will look like a bored millionaire, and you cannot blame people for the fact that they will want a piece of you.

On the other hand, when you have just a normal looking motorcycle, people will know that you are an adventurer and will automatically change their mind. You might disagree with this statement, but it doesn't matter; this is simple human behavior.

N: 2 - If you want to travel cheaply you will need a tent.

It will be your mobile home and could save you hundreds of dollars. In relation to the number one affordable motorcycle, I will add just one more question:

What is the logic, to spend 20,000$ for a bike and more than 2,000$ for gear, and at the end to sleep in a tent? For this amount of money, you can go around half of the world and pay only for hotels. Anyway, everybody is different, and we have different preferences, so let's go back to the tent.

Buy a tent for two, even if you are traveling alone. The comfort of the double tent will convince you to use it more often. The more you use it, the cheaper the trip will become. Especially if you can camp for free. In a single, one-man tent, it will be like you are in a coffin. Next time, you will just go to a hotel. Do not ask how I came to this conclusion.

Of course in some countries, the hotels are so cheap that it isn't really worth it to camp, but this is a different story.

N: 3 – Travel as lightly as possible.

I have said this many times, but I will say it again – Weight always matters! More luggage is equal to more bags; hard cases or whatever luggage system you have. Bulky saddlebags or even worse, hard cases, will increase your consumption rate by about 0.5l per 100km. On a 10,000km trip, this is about 100 euro, not much, but piece by piece, as you travel, you will come to some serious numbers.

Another very valid point to think about is that when you travel light, you are only taking the most important stuff, which automatically reduces the need of buying expensive adventure gadgets, which as we all know, are not cheap.

When the bike is light, the petrol consumption is at least 1 litter less, and the life of the tires are usually 10 to 20% longer. It is the same with oils, brake pads, the chain, and many more. From a long term perspective, this is all money saved.

N: 4 – Reduce speed.

I don't have to tell you that when you ride fast, your motorcycle consumes more petrol. A fast speed also eats the tires much faster than you can ever imagine. Again, it is not much, but when you add it to the first few points it becomes a noticeable price. Do not forget, that on the longer trips, the constant speed is what really matters. Reducing the speed will also minimize the chances of an accident and as we know, this can be very expensive or even worse, to get hurt or die.

N: 5 – Buy food from supermarkets.

Is really depends on your budget, but f you want to do it as cheaply as possible, this will help you a lot. The prices in the restaurants and the shops are usually very different. For example, in Europe, a nice meal in an average restaurant will cost you about 15-20 euro. If you spend this amount in the supermarket, you will have food for at least three days.

N: 6 – Use hostels instead of hotels.

Even in the hostels, you can have a private room if this is what you looking for, but there, you will be able to cook your food, and this will reduce the price significantly. Also in the hostels, you will meet many nice people, and you can receive some really useful advice and directions to help with your logistics, this will also lower your costs.

N: 7 – Always stop riding before sunset.

This will help you to have enough time to find a proper place to sleep. In the middle of the night, after spending all day riding, you will be happy to pay any price just to have a bed to sleep. Here, I am talking from my own experience.

N: 8 – Plan ahead.

The logistics of your travel is something very important. Plan everything ahead. I really respect the people who travel without any preparations, but I prefer to be ready. By doing your route in advance, you can minimize the km and the time you need to spend on the road.

The example I will give you now is from my last trip to South Asia. The original plan was to travel with my motorcycle, but later, because of the changes in the Iranian custom regime, I took the decision to fly there and use local bikes instead of riding my own. With the first plan, to ride there, I would need at least 45 days and around 1,500 dollars (petrol, hotels, road tax, and food), just to reach India. This was only the price to get there! I would probably need the same to go back, to ride or to ship the bike to Europe.

The worst part of everything was the time, and as you know, time costs money. In the best scenario, I would need 3 months and 3,000 Dollars to get there and back, and then I have to pay for all the expenses for the time that I am going to spend in those countries.

What I did instead was to fly there and use the local bikes. Yes, it might be much better to have my motorcycle there, but at what cost? For your information, all the flight tickets I bought: Berlin – Karachi(Pakistan), Islamabad (Pakistan) – Mumbai(India), Kolkata(India) – Dhaka(Bangladesh) and Dhaka(Bangladesh) – and then back to Berlin cost me around 1,600 Dollars. This was twice as cheap as the first plan, without even the additional cost of the time I needed to spend there.

What was best of all, is that I did the trip for 2 months instead of 5 and saw much more than I could have done with the first option. This is just one example, but I have many like this.

N: 9 – Prepare the bike before the trip.

Do everything before the trip. Change the tires, oils, filters, bearings, cables. Basically you have to change everything that has a possiblity to fail during the trip. Even if you still have some miles due before the next oil change or the tires could have more 2,000km, change it before the trip. This will eliminate the need for doing it during the trip, which is not always possible at the prices you are used to paying. For example, in Kazakhstan, the price of the tires was almost three times higher than the price of exactly the same tires in Europe. Of course, you cannot predict everything, but at least you can try...

N: 10 – Think outside of the box.

Be creative and try to find new solutions for every possible problem you might need to face. Remember:

'The bike is just a tool, the travel is what really matters!'

Do not pay too much attention to the bike, instead of that, focus on the trip itself. Enjoy every moment, be friendly with every person you see on the road, and the world will be always open for you!

In relation to everything I just said, I have another chapter for you:

How to go around the world without robbing a bank?

Okay, it is clear how to go on a single trip, but to go around the world is a different story. It is a dream for many motorcycle riders, but how do you do it without the need to rob a bank? This is was the question that I had many years ago, and I found one very simple solution. Of course, it is not a secret, and I am happy to share my thoughts, and I really hope that they will help you!

I guess that you expect me to tell you some clichés like finding a sponsor, collect money from donations or raise a Facebook campaign, if every one of your friends gives you just 10$ it will be enough…just stop, okay! It doesn't work like that! You might have thousands of followers on Facebook, Instagram, Twitter or Youtube, but it doesn't mean that they will be ready to give even a single dollar for you!

If you want to be noticed from sponsors or somebody to spend money on you, first you have to prove yourself.

'It is very simple, but how do you do it when you have no money to travel?'

It is like paragraph 22. You need to travel to prove yourself, but you don't have money to travel!

Another option will be to quit your job, sell everything and go around the world by motorcycle, it sounds like a great adventure, right? I am sure that it is actually, no questions about it, but how many of you could take this decision?

Even I had this idea at some stage. I actually calculated everything, and I was almost ready to do it. Now I am glad that I didn't!

The problem was, that being a responsible husband and father, like many of you, this was not an easy decision. To put on a scale, everything you have, simply in the name of the adventure is a bit… I would say different. More, I thought better I realized the negatives of such a trip. Let me explain to you with more details:

Everything started as you know with Charlie Bormann and Ewan McGregor. They made this great trip 'The long way around' and completely changed the way it should be done. Of course, there were many others before that, but they were the first who actually showed everything on camera.

This trip was like the spark I needed to light my fire. Anyway, even though their journey was great, they saw one very small part of the world. Actually, it was 20,000 miles crossing the globe from west to east. The idea I had was much bigger than that. I was planning to go to all 5 continents and visit as many countries as I possibly could.

Regarding my calculations at that time, I came to the conclusion that I would need at least one year and no less than 45,000 $. To sort out the finance part of the trip, I was ready to sell some of the properties I had, and pray that the rest will come from somewhere. The money was okay, but the time schedule, the whole year, this was a different story.

Most of you know how difficult is to convince our wives for us to be able to go on a trip for month or two, thanks to the great system I had, it worked without any problem for me, but one year is something completely different. Let's say that I can manage to do this as well, the biggest question 'Am I taking the right decision?' is still there!

To leave family, the business and everything I had was an impossible task for me, and I guess that it will be the same for many of you. As I said before, many people do this it, but I was not brave enough, and I didn't have the courage to do it.

Because it was my dream, and as you know, I never give up my dreams, I realised that I needed to make another plan. There are no problems only solutions. So, instead of trying to do it all at once, I decided to go on a number of different, smaller trips.

I was thinking then, and now I am completely sure that this way, we have many more advantages than the original plan. Let me give you more details about what the benefits of doing it this way are:

1. *This will give you the time to prepare the bike and yourself much better. Very important if you want to have trouble-free trips.*

2. *The option to go on each trip with the proper machine. Again, this will help you to make the trip much, cheaper, easier, and safer of course.*

3. *Possibility to learn from the mistakes and correct them for the next trip. To gain priceless experience.*

4. *Time to think and make better routes. Things are constantly changing, some roads are closed, new ones are built, the political situation is changing in some countries and much more.*

5. *More time for your family. I don't have to explain how important it is.*

6. *The possibility to save money for the next trip. Money is the engine of the world!*

7. *A great opportunity to make strong friendships with many people around the world. This will help you more than you can imagine.*

8. *The possibility to change the plan at any moment if you need to. Unexpected circumstances, for example, the death of a family member or some serious health problem.*

9. The option to stop for a year or even two if you have to. To complete something more important for you or for your family.

10. Number ten is the most interesting, at least for me. It is the possibility to create your own brand and transfer your motorcycle passion to a full-time profession.

Yes, exactly, you can convert your hobby to a real profession.

What a dream to ride your bike around the world and get paid for that too!

I know that now you will ask me **HOW?** This is the million dollar question, isn't it?

Unfortunately, at this stage, I will not give you the answer. I have a plan to make an online video course about how to do it. Step by step. It will contain only real and proven advice. Everything that I will share will be from my own experiences.

Actually, everything is already in my head. I know the exact steps because it has already worked for me, but I need more time to set the wheels in motion for this next project.

You might ask: **'If you know it already, why do you have to wait?'**

Because right now, it is too early, and you are not going to believe it. I can do it at whatever moment I decide to, but without the real data, without the real proof that it works, it will be just one super exciting dream. Next year, I will be able to show you some real numbers to support my words.

Just to summarise everything that I have said, in the past ten years I have been to more than 60 countries. Of course, I still have many more to explore, but I am on the right track. You might say – Yes, it is easy for you!

Easy? What you are talking about? Do you think that I am a single bored millionaire who just needs to decide where to go?

My friend, I am an ordinary person like you. I have a family, kids, and all the needs you have. I was born and raised in a communistic country that most of you even don't know the name! I have needed to start my life from scratch three times over. I know very well what it means to have no money or possibilities, I know exactly how you might feel at this moment. Most of you, I mean people from the west, cannot understand how I felt back in the time, but I never gave up my dreams. They were like my engine, my guiding light and the only way out! Keep dreaming my friend and never give up!

Here you are again; I converted this chapter to a motivational speech! I am what I am, and I really hope that this will help you to take the steps you need to turn your dreams into real adventures!

*****

The secrets nobody ever tells you!

This is a really provocative title isn't it? Now you are curious. What are the secrets? Of course, I will tell you everything you need to know, just keep reading!

Most of the things I am going to share with you are very logical, but nobody ever talks about it. Yes, the motorcycle trips are something great, and I still believe that this is the best way to see the world, but you really need to be aware of what to expect. You have to be ready to face reality, not only the fun factor. Otherwise you might be very disappointed.

In this chapter, I am not going to discourage from what you are about to do, the idea is to open your eyes and prepare you even better. As I said many times:

'The preparation is the key to success!'

Alright, let's talk about the top secrets that nobody ever tells you:

1. When you get home, you will remember the trip, not the bike.

A bike is just a tool, the travel is what really matters. Do you know that at the moment, I am riding a Yamaha XT 660 Z, 2008? If yes, you are one of only 20 people who are aware of this. Most of the people around the world have never heard about this brand and model, but they watch my channel. What they know is my face and some of my trips. Yes, today I have a Yamaha, but tomorrow it could be something else, just like I did in my last trip to South Asia. In Pakistan, I rode Benelli TNT 25 (250cc) in India and Nepal Royal Enfield Himalayan and in Bangladesh it was a Lifan KPT (150cc).

I am not married to the Yamaha family! It is just the tool I use at the moment. Focus on the trip and on the important moments there, not on the bike. Stop comparing yourself with others. There will be always someone with a better bike or more money than you. It is a motorcycle trip – your motorcycle trip, it is not a competition! In relation to this, I will tell you about the second most important thing:

2. The gear is just gear: It is there to help you to complete the trip.

Correct, the gear is designed to help, not to make you a better rider. Do not even think that because you have paid for an expensive jacket or some kind of golden helmet, this will make your trip much better than someone with budget options!

I am not saying that you have to go with the cheap stuff, no absolutely not, buy whatever you can afford. What I am trying to say is that the experience you are going to have on your journey depends on many other circumstances and even the best gear cannot guarantee that!

3. **You will have some really bad moments.**

I am not talking about accidents or breakdown situations. That is far too obvious! I am talking about something more touchable.

- You will miss your family and friends so much. You will ask yourself, what I am doing here? Why the hell have I come to the end of the world? What I am looking for?

- There will be some days when you will doubt everything. Moments when nothing goes the way you have planned it to be. When it will feel like the whole world will be against you!

- I am sure that on some of your trips, you will want to quit, but you won't have this chance, because you will be so far away…

To make it even worse, I will tell you that you might start to think about stopping riding altogether.

4. **People don't care about your trips.**

Many of you still believe that if you go on an adventure trip, this will get you noticed. You think that all of your friends, and their friends, and everybody around the world will care about your journey!

Well, I am here to disappoint you and let you know that except for your family members, no one really cares about you. People are too busy living their lives, and what might be interesting and important for you, might not be the same for them.

For example, you may have just come back from two months of a very difficult adventure trip and have a meeting with friends. One of them talks about you to the others:

'He just come back from a great adventure trip around the Himalayas!'

And the other guy said:

'Ohh cool! Listen, what was the name of the girl we met last night?…'

Can you see what I mean? Even your family is not going to be so enthusiastic to listen to your stories. The life clock is ticking. You have to go on a trip for yourself, and not for someone else! This is the only way to really enjoy it and take all the positives from it. Make sure you are taking the trip for the right reasons.

For example I always go to the places I want to see, and I always do this in the way I want to, regardless of what others will say. I know what I want to see on my trips and what I don't want to see. I know that the Alps are a great motorcycle riding destination, but they have never really been so attractive for me. Sure, it might be nice to see it once or twice, but that's it.

What is good for one could be a disaster for another! Just remember this.

5. To complete any trip, you have to sacrifice a lot of things.

There are many, but I will point out here just some of the most obvious things:

- *Internet access. There will be many moments, even days without it. Some people are not ready for that, and they could have a real panic at the thought of life without connectivity.*

- *You have to forget about the nice dinner and TV every night.*

- *You might not have access to a shower every day. It could very easily become a week or more…*

I will tell you a funny Bulgarian story:

A young Journalist was taking an interview from an old man who was living in a very small village. No water, no power, he actually lived in conditions that were very similar to life in the 19th Century. So he asked the man:

> *'With all due respect to your lifestyle, I do not see any shower – what do you do?'*

The old man said:

> *'Oh, this is not a problem, I just go to the river.'*

The journalist was confused: 'Ok, but what about during the winter?'

'The winter is short – I don't even worry about it.'

I hope that you get the point. If this is not a problem for you as well, then all good.

Ok, this was funny, but there are some serious things:

- *Your relation, family, and kids. Yes, if you think that your family will love that you are planning to be missing for a month or more – you are wrong! –they will miss you and worry so much about you, this could be really painful for them.*

- *Your work. One way or another, it will be affected. Even if you have somebody to replace you, the results are not going to be the same. The same story applies to your income sources. Believe me, I know this from* my own experience. Even though I am the boss, because I have my own business, it is still the same.

So my friend, after everything I have just said, if you still want to go I can say only one thing:

Welcome to my adventure world!

Once you test this drug, you will become hooked for the rest of your life! It doesn't matter how tough it is going to be, you will always come back for more.

*****

How to travel and stay alive?

This question always concerned me, from the very moment I took my first trip. It is a very important topic, for the obvious reason that you need to stay alive, but also, because you have to remove some old habits and learn some new ones. After that, you need to practice until they become a way of thinking or as we call them 'second nature'.

In this chapter, I will give you 5 very practical tips about how to travel the world and always come back home safe, and in one piece.

I guess that now, you will expect me to tell you some secret riding techniques, but I might disappoint you, and tell you that I don't have this in mind. I will try to explain as simply as possible what I do, and how this always help me to come back home safely and in one piece.

I believe that when we try to convince someone, the personal experience is worth more than thousands of hard to pronounce words and the typical clichés you may have already heard many times before. So, no riding techniques or special gear, just me and my thoughts!

Oooo, you are still here, great! I appreciate that! Keep reading, and I promise that at the end, you will get what you need.

Tip N: 1 – Never put yourself in a situation you cannot handle alone.

Let me explain what I mean: Even if you are in a group, always do what you believe is right, or your skills will allow you to do. Do not try to imitate or match the others as you might be treading on very thin ice and finish things really badly.

You are a different person; you have a different riding style and maybe even a different bike. What is easy for one could be a complete nightmare for another. Do not rely on the group to help you in any situation and make sure you always try to stay in control.

While I know that the motorcycle community is strong, I also know that if you fell down and broke your leg, they will help you to get to the hospital, but then you need to do it alone, and you will have to deal with the pain, the shame, and the problems after that. On the other hand, their journey will continue with or without you. Ride your bike the way you ride it when you are alone. I hope that you get the point now.

Tip N: 2 – Travel alone or with a maximum of one friend.

Many people will disagree with me on this point, but it doesn't matter. I know myself, and I am 100% convinced on this point. Let me give you a couple of examples:

- When you travel in a group, you risk so much more. Why? Because you will always try to catch them in the traffic, on the highway, or even worse on the twisty roads. Sometimes, you will take a risky decision just because of that fact. Riding too fast or making a dangerous overtaking manoeuvre just to keep up.

- Even if you are in a leading position, you need to watch the mirrors much more than normal. Just to make sure that everybody is behind you as they should be, and this will move your attention from the important things in front of you. I have experienced this many times, and I confess that I needed to take unnecessary risks, just to follow the group or to wait for them.

- Not everyone is able to ride without stops for two hours, but when you are in a group, you might have to. This could lead you to unexpected fatigue and of course, to an even more serious danger that could cause an accident.

- Bad or not, respectable behaviour of group member could put all of you in a not so pleasant or even a risky situation. I have experienced this as well. You might be a great person, but not everyone is like you.

- The difference in the engine size could bring serious conflicts after couple of days. For example, if you ride 600cc, but some of the others have 1200cc.

There are many more examples of why I make this point, but I think that these are enough. So, my opinion is, that the safest way to travel is alone or with one person. If you are doing it with another person, try to find something who has a similar riding style, budget, and engine size. This will make things much easier and more simple.

Tip N: 3 – Always wear full motorcycle gear.

I know that you have heard this many times before, but most of you never listen! I keep seeing people riding their motorcycles with hiking or even with army boots on, they say that they do this because of the comfort. You have to understand one simple truth:

'Comfort and protection never work together!'

I am not even going to discuss the situations in Asia where people don't know what proper protection really is. I am sure that you have seen motorcycle crashes on YouTube. Usually, the rider flies in the air like a small puppet and when he hits the ground or the other vehicle, the results are never good. Even if you have on the full motorcycle gear, the chances to stay alive are very small. Can you imagine what it would be without it? Don't play this game or take this gamble because sooner or later you will lose!

On my last trip to South Asia, there were many times when we finished the ride for the day, undressed, took a shower, then after a couple of hours, we decided to go out to eat something or to visit the local shop. Because these places would never be within walking distance, we would usually take the bikes. Regardless, I would always dress in my gear, and the local guys would say:

 'No, you don't need it, it is just 5 km and so on …'

My question is:

'And what, because you are going to ride for 5 km, if you go down you are not going to be hurt, is that right?

'No, but we will ride slowly...'

And just a few minutes into the journey, they twist the throttle even more. Even in the City, where the risks to have an accident is much higher than riding on the highway. The common perception is, that on the highway – full gear – in the city no need to dress.

I had one similar discussion with one young boy in Pakistan, and at the end, I asked him:

'I am 44 years old, I have ridden motorcycles for many years and I have never had a serious accident, do you know why?'

He asked: 'Why?'

'Because I never ride like you, that's why? With your riding style and without any gear, sooner or later you will be hurt.'

You don't need to learn this the hard way. Always wear the full motorcycle gear! I will repeat, **MOTORCYCLE GEAR**! Army or hiking boots, a leather jacket or jeans might be a good outfit, but they are not motorcycle gear!

Tip N: 4 – You are not a great rider, you have been lucky.

I am tired of listening to people about how great riders they think they are; and about how they have been to so many places, about how they rode these fast and dangerous roads, and about the fact that they have so much experience. They speak of how they see everything and they cannot be surprised because they have been riding from many years and their instincts are on a different level; they will talk about how they feel the danger in advance, and how they are able to eliminate it without any problems and so on and so on…

I also have heard a lot of stories like this:

'I have been to the Alps many times, I have been to Asia, Africa, South America…I have 100, 200, 500 thousand one million km under my belt!'

…and what? Does this make you a superman? No, you have been a lucky guy!

Usually, accidents will happen when you really believe that you are in control of everything. The situations on the road and off the road are so many that our entire life is not enough to experience them all!

You are never ready. Every time I jump on the bike, I learn something new, no exception. You are the same. Once you accept that, your chances to stay alive will increase significantly.

Tip N: 5 – Ride the bike you can control.

Okay, this sounds very obvious and logical, but let me tell you a story:

I met one very interesting nice guy in India. We talked about bikes and he told me that he has an idea to upgrade his motorcycle. He was riding a 150cc Hero. It's a dual sport bike, Indian brand. He was thinking to go with the same model, but a 200cc version; I was surprised and asked him:

'Why you don't go for at least 250 or 300cc? This 200cc is about the same as yours. After just a couple of months, you will surely need more.'

He replied to me, with very serious tone:

'Because until now, I only rode a 150cc light motorcycle. My skills are on that level. I am not sure that I am ready for something bigger.'

At the beginning, I was planning to say to him that it's about the same and he can easily shift to something bigger, but then I said:

'Yes, you are right. It will be a nice step to have and to polish your skills.'

Here in Europe, everybody is focused on big and powerful bikes – 1000cc, 1200cc, 1250cc or 1290 100H:P 150H.P 200H.P …

Some of the riders I have seen do not have the experience and the skills to control even 25 H.P. So, why do they have it? I don't know, you tell me?

Ride the bike that you can control in any situation. On both good or bad roads. Dry or wet asphalt, road or off road. Mud, sand or gravel. If you cannot, learn how to do it, practice until you get enough confidence to go alone. Do not push yourself or compare yourself with others. You are a unique person and you can have your unique experience, no matter what you ride.

Bonus tip: Always trust your sixth sense.

Your internal voice, guardian angel or whatever you want to name it; I always listen what it says. It is usually the first thing that comes into my mind when I have a risky situation. Sometimes it is completely different from the normal logic, but the result is always good for me.

*****

What I learned from my trips?

Many years ago, a friend of mine told me that nothing was worth more than to travel around the world. I completely agree with this statement and since then, I have never stopped travelling and even tried to teach my kids how important this is. So far, they have learned something, but I am not sure that they really get the whole idea, yet. Sometimes, I create interesting lessons at home, asking them about different places around the world, I show them pictures and try to provoke their curiosity. It doesn't always work, but at least I am trying.

In this chapter, I will try to do something similar with you. Of course, I am not going to ask about your geography skills, but I will tell you about the most important lessons that I have learned from my trips. Let's get started!

So, if you like the risk and the adventures, then you can start travelling as soon as possible with the idea to see the world. You can do it with or without any money. It has been proven by many people already.

On the other hand, if you go to Oxford, Stanford, Kenbridge, or any other big and famous university, then you will learn a lot and get a professional degree, which will probably ensure that you get a good job, decent money, and if you are lucky enough, you might have some free time for travelling and who knows, you might even get to see the world...

Have you seen the paradox? With the first option, you will see the world, with the second you might see the world!

With this, I am not trying to say that to have a professional degree is a bad thing, no absolutely not; what I am trying to say is that you have to see the world. This is the only way to understand it!

As you already know, I love philosophic discussions, but I won't waste any more from your time and will go straight to the point:

What are the most important lessons I have learned from my trips?

N: 1 – The world is so big, but the time that we have on earth is so little!

I am sure that you have heard some of the phrases:

- Don't worry, you have enough time…
- Now is not the right moment…
- First, I have to finish this or complete that…
- Nothing is more important than a good education…
- A family is more important than your dreams…
- You have responsibilities and many more…

Before I continue, let me tell you one real story:

A friend of mine worked for a big international company. Once every couple of years, the company would pay for a Psychologist to talk with people and see if they have any problems. A couple of years ago, the Psychologist asked him to describe his life from the beginning until the present moment.

Being a serious and organized man, he did it with great detail and described everything in written form over 4-5 pages: How he finished in the school that his parents found for him, how he got married, bought an apartment, built a house, a family business, family vacations, what he did his wife, his kids, and so on…

When he finished, the Psychologist said:

'Wow! I did not expect such a detailed explanation but thank you, it was great. I have only one question: Where are you in the whole picture?'

He tried to explain that he was there all the time, but she repeated the question, and this time she said:

'I know that you have done everything for your parents, your family, and the business, but what you have done for you?'

He was confused and said:

'I believed that I did the right things…'

She clarified things for him:

'Yes, I understand this and you have done well, but you also need to know that this is your life and you don't need to sacrifice it for others!'

'Aaaaaa! I never thought of it this way'… he said, and soon after that he bought a motorcycle and started traveling around the world.

I know that many wives, including mine will hate me now, but this is the reality!

Do not rely on the notion that there will be a proper time or that you can do it later. The world is a big place and there is never enough time. Old people never regret the things that they have done; it is more so the things what they didn't. Keep that in mind!

N: 2 – A bike is just a tool, the travel is what really matters!

I am sure that you have heard me saying this many times, even in this book, this is because I really mean it. After you complete the trip, you will remember so many different things: people, places, views, weather, road conditions, food or whatever you have seen there, but I really doubt that you will remember how the bike performed on that hill, how the suspension absorbed the holes, how the windshield protected your chest or how the fog lights provided 20% more light…

Before you attack me with your arguments, let me tell you something:

I know that all of these things are important, especially on long trips, but I also know that we can easily do it without. People rode motorcycles around the world many years before these so-called necessary adventure things even existed. I really hope that you will understand this because the best adventure motorcycle is the one you have in the garage! It is much better to travel with whatever you have at the moment, than to stay at home and wait for the perfect adventure machine!

N: 3 – People are great, and there is nothing scary about travelling.

I know that the political situation around the world is not so clear, and the news makes it even worse, but all of this shouldn't stop you. A one month trip, taken somewhere different from your country will give you more information than years spent in front of the TV or in the library. It will open your eyes, and you will see the world in different colors, and from an entirely new perspective.

It will be so powerful and so clear that you will be addicted forever. You will realize that we are all the same and that we all desire the same things. Yes, we might have different skin colors or believe in different Gods, but anything else is practically the same.

N: 4 – Travelling is not that expensive.

It is hard to believe this, but many of you will realize that it is cheaper to travel with motorcycle than living in big cities. Here I expect you to say: Pavlin, even when you travel you need to pay your bills!

Yes, this is true, but I don't need to pay the petrol and the parking for my car, coffees or food that is triple the price, fancy restaurants, cinemas, shopping, ice cream for the kids, and the usual city expenses. When you draw the line, you will start laughing, seriously. Even if you have to pay a bit more, you will never regret it – I promise you!

N: 5 – When you travel you, will appreciate what you have!

I always say to my wife that she needs to come with me, at least once, just to realize how happy she is! Travelling will make you calmer, happier, and a much better person than you can even imagine!

You have to see the world to be able to appreciate what you have. I know that many wives or husbands are worried that this will ruin your relationships, but it is actually the other way around. After every trip, you will come home recharged with so many positive feelings that she or he will feel it, will love you, and will always let you go again!

I know that all of these things might just sound like just nice speech, but as I said, it has taken me many years to realize the simple truth behind these words. Do not be like me, make something, take some action, go ride, see the world, and you will never regret it!

*****

What are you doing wrong?

We make mistakes because we don't have experience; and the experience only comes from the mistakes we have made! What a paradox! Again we have the famous paragraph 22, a never-ending circle, isn't it? In this chapter, I will talk about the 5 things that you are probably doing wrong. Keep reading!

As you know, nobody is perfect, there is no doubt about it. From the mistakes, we make, we are actually learning. Just to make it clear from the beginning, I will tell that I don't have any goals to teach you, convince you or push you to change your riding style or the habits that you already have. The idea is merely to inform you, to expose the weak points of some of your choices, and to show you a different perspective.

I know that with some of what I am going to say, you will agree, but some of you will it hard to swallow, especially with number 5. No worries, I am okay with all of this. The final decision to believe or not will be yours, and I cannot take any responsibility for it. Enough talking, let's go to the mistakes:

N:1 – Overpacking.

This is a classic mistake for every new rider, the feeling that you will forget something. Do not even worry about it, it is absolutely normal, and we have all had it at one time or another. The example I can give you now is to pack 7 t-shirts, 7 pairs of socks and 7 sets of underwear for a one week trip. Sounds logic, right? But what are you going to do if the trip is 2 months, you going to load 60 t-shirts, socks, and pants? You don't have to! Even in the middle of nowhere, you will be able to wash your clothes.

The second example is to take too many tools, just because you might need it. Instead, a simple kit with the most important stuff is more than enough because if you have a serious technical problem, you will need a garage anyway.

The third example is too many electronics and cables. To carry, computer, tablet, iPod, and telephone at the same time. 20 different charging cables and USB cables, and many more for what? Are you going to ride or will you work all the time? Believe or not, but after closer inspection and removing the unnecessary items, your luggage weight will drop by 50%. The weight always matters! Remember it, and you will avoid so many unnecessary problems.

N: 2 – Eat too much.

Many riders complain that they have a problem trying to stay awake for more than 2 hours, especially on the long boring highways. A few people have even asked me what I do to prevent this. Again this is a classic mistake, and it's coming from not understanding how our bodies work. Most of you believe that food gives us energy, which is absolutely true, but first, the food needs to be digested. It usually takes anything between 2 to 8 hours, depending on the type of food you consume. During that process, our body needs a lot of energy. When you eat too much, you actually give your body so much work to do, that anything else doesn't really matter, because the food is the priority. Wait until the evening before you start for big steaks or any heavy meals.

N: 3 – Breaks that are too long.

To stop for an hour or more is not a really good idea. What I notice about my trips is that the first hour or two are the most challenging to ride. I usually think about how much more travel I have ahead, I will constantly check the time, and the mileage I set for the day looks almost impossible. I cannot find a proper position or always need to adjust mirrors and so on, but after a couple of hours I am entering the so-called riding mode, and everything becomes so easy and natural. Actually, after just 500km, I feel much better than the first 100km. I am not joking; this is absolutely true.

The problem is, that when you make a long break, you actually exit from that riding mode and need to start again. Another very good reason not to do it is that it doesn't matter how fast you going to ride after that, your average speed will drop significantly. Stop for a coffee, let's say for just 30 minutes, and this will actually help you gain one hour in your overall riding time. I am not going into science debates over this, why not just try it for yourself, and you will see the result. From my experience, 15 minutes to refill the tank and grab a sandwich is more than enough.

N: 4 – Having a full rain suit instead of two parts.

Which rain gear is better; two parts or one? Technically, the full suit protects you much better, because you don't have the open gap between the jacket and the pants, but, (here you are again the important BUT), it is difficult to wear it, especially when the rain has already started and you are under a small bridge on the highway. You will jump like a chicken there trying to get in it quickly.

With two parts, it is without a doubt, much easier. It will also give you the possibility to wear it separately. For example, on cold mornings, I use the jacket as extra wind protection, or on muddy terrain, I can have only the pants to keep my riding pants clear. Another question: Do I need boot covers? Yes, nothing is 100% waterproof. Even the best boots will give up after a couple of hour's heavy rain. So yes, you need boot covers.

N: 5 – Having a top case.

Wow, I shouldn't say that! Now I expect you to slap me in the face with the arguments that this is not true! You will try to explain to me that this is the most convenient thing on your motorcycle. You can even store your helmet in it...

Yes yes yes, this is actually the only plus I can find of having a top case – it is convenient. Everything else makes no sense at all. Once again: I don't have any goals to change your riding gear or style, I just will tell you some simple facts:

1. During some of your trips, it will break. The reasons why yours is still in one piece are few:

   - It is made from very strong materials, which means that it is too heavy, even when empty.
   - You never ride anything different than nice smooth asphalt roads.
   - Because you just don't have enough trips.

2. Because of the false security it gives you, it is more likely that you will leave the bike unattended.

- What you have to know, is that the lock it has is very similar to the locks we have in our post boxes. It could be easily opened with a simple screwdriver.
- The last is that because of the extra luggage space, you will take some useless stuff. If you don't believe me, check what you have inside now!

3. And last but not least, is the ergonomics of your bike.

Motorcycle companies spend thousands of dollars each year to make amazing machines. The engineers need to test every detail in many different situations, even in wind tunnels in order to ensure that it has the perfect shape. They spend so many hours on finding the right balance between weight and power. They pay great attention to a low center of gravity, weight distribution, and many more factors.

After the model is ready, they start the test rides. On the track, on the normal roads, and off-road, if necessary. Again, the company needs to be certain that everything works absolutely perfectly and trouble-free. The final product is like a piece of art, or at least some of the models on the market are.

So far so good until here, and you will agree with me, but then comes the new owner of that piece of art – you, and you will decide that the top case will be nice to have because it is convenient! Completely ignoring all the science involved to create this perfect machine. What a punch in the company's face!

Fair enough, it is your bike, and you know what is best for you!

What you don't know, is that by adding this additional 5 or 10 kg on the tail of your bike, you are actually saying to the factory:

'You know what, I know much better than you!'

So maybe you don't care about it, but keep reading, because now I will tell you something interesting, and it is something that you need to know because it concerns your safety.

By adding additional weight on the tail, you actually take some weight from the front wheel. You can prove this example. Lift your bike on the center stand and press the rear side of the bike. What you will see is that the front will go into the air. When you ride, the wind forces press the top box and cause even more of a negative impact on the front.

When you have bad road conditions, like wet asphalt or even ice, this could be a really dangerous situation. It is worse when we have a bumpy road. Each time when you hit a big hole, the heavy rear lifts the front tire from the ground. It is just for a couple of mm, but it's enough to lose traction and have an accident.

This effect also depends on the speed, the faster you ride, the stronger the wind force will be, and the worse the situation becomes.

Here, of course, I expect the logical question:

'Okay, if all of this is true, why do the big manufacturers like BMW, Yamaha, Suzuki, Honda, and many more offer top boxes for almost each one of the touring models?'

Because they have a huge marketing department and they know exactly what you will want to buy; and they are more than happy to sell it to you. The adventure market is growing very fast. More and more people will jump on it in the next couple of years. Almost everybody will come to the idea of having a top box, and all because it is **'convenient'**!

It is already calculated and proven that in the long-term, buyers will spend more money on accessories and aftermarket upgrades than they actually spend on the original bike purchase. Why are they still selling cigarettes or junk food? Do you believe that someone needs it?

There actually just a few models on the market which are designed with stock hard panniers and top cases, like the BMW 1600, Triumph Trophy or Honda Goldwin, for any other model it is utter nonsense!

As I said at the start, I did not expect anything from you. You can agree or disagree with what I just mentioned. It is your bike, your trip, and your life. I am just the messenger, and I will be more than happy if this information helps even just one person to take the right decision.

******

5 Things that I wish I knew when I started.

If you still haven't started with traveling, you probably will have already heard the phrase:

'It is never too late to start touring around the world.'

Many of you thought that there was more than enough time. That there are many other important things that you have to complete first before you decide to go. Sounds very logical, but the reality is different. What I am about to tell you now, are the top 5 things that I wish I would have known when I started with my motorcycle trips.

I have to use another famous phrase:

'The world is so big, but the time we have on earth is so little!'

There are 195 countries in the world at the moment. 195 different perspectives, 195 points of views, and actually, it is like 195 different worlds. I don't know about you, but I have always been a curious person. When I was a kid, my father bought the world atlas for me and my big brother. It was a very expensive hardcover book. I don't know how much exactly he paid for it, but the price was nothing compared to the priceless information it provides. I was spending so much time looking at the beautiful color pages, dreaming that one day I will go there.

I always loved geography and maps. Even today, I have a lot of them at home. When I have nothing to do, I would look at it and make some new plans. Anyway, the times are changed, and now it is so easy to travel around the world.

As I said, it was my dream, but now, I am the person who wrote this book. I am the one who talks with you right now, and I am more than happy to share my thoughts with anyone who wants to listen.

The old people said:

'Be careful what you wish for because it might come true!'

As usual, I talk too much; now let's go to the things I promised.

N: 1 - There is no proper time.

Maybe you believe that now it is not the proper time. The trips could wait until you build your house, until the kids finish school, the business gets better, when you start to earn more money, when the company gives you the promised bonus or when you finally get the new job you are looking for. There are so many reasons or excuses to stop you. So-called **'more important things'** or whatever you want to name it.

I will agree with this, sometimes we do what we have to do. WE have our responsibilities, but let me ask you something….

'Are you feeling happy with the life you have now? Don't you want to see the world, to experience something different?'

If the answer is:' Yes, I am happy with the current situation.' I perfectly understand and respect that, not everyone is born with a needle in the ass, as my father used to say.

But if the answer is: ' No!' What you are waiting for? A proper time? It will never come, and your dreams will always stay somewhere in the future.

N: 2 – The most important part of any trip is you.

I constantly repeat this again and again! It is not about the bike, it is not about the gear, it is not about the destination, it is not even about the trip itself! It is all about your the experience and the great moments you are going to have on that journey. The people that you going to meet, the unforgettable situations, and the unique views you going to see there. All of these will stick in your memory and actually, they will change your life forever. Every trip will give you something, and you will come home a changed and a better person! You will be a better partner, a better father or the friend everyone wants to have. If this is not a reason to start with the trips as soon as possible, then I don't know what would be!

N: 3 – There are no problems only solutions.

Yes, exactly, for every possible problem you will find at least three solutions. There are no things like the perfect plan or 100% safety. This is a myth! An illusion that makes us feel better and step into the unknown with more confidence.

'Yes, Pavlin, you are right; but motorcycle trips are still a dangerous hobby, aren't they?'

True, but you can have car accident while going to your safe 9 to 5 job or get hit by a brick falling down from some construction work when you come back from the supermarket. The truth is, that even our normal everyday activities could become a real adventure, and nobody knows what the future looks like!

N: 4 – Plan more time instead of more kilometres.

I wish I would have known this when I started. I did so many trips for a shorter time. Spending less time than I should. This is something you really need to consider when you make your plans. Every day, which one you spend on the highways riding to the next point is like a nothing day, unless you are not a competitor of Iron buts or something similar.

I had some trips that if I have to make again, I will definitely add much more time on, and I will try to see as much as possible. This is, maybe one of the reasons why I completely changed my trip to India, and I can tell you now, I am so happy that I did it.

N: 5 – I know nothing.

Many riders will consider themselves to be a great motorcyclist or very important travelers. They believe that the experience they have will help them in any situation or that nothing can surprise them.

Well… I am here to confess, that the more I ride, the better I realize that I know nothing. Every time when I jump on the bike, I learn something new. It is like a never-ending school or a forever student. Don't lie to yourself by thinking that you are a super professional, because you are not. It doesn't matter how many bikes you had or how many miles you have. The situations on the road or off-road are so many, that even 10 lives won't be enough to experience them all and to be ready for everything. The faster you understand this, the better chances you have to stay alive.

*****

How to stay motivated on long trips?

It is easy to stay motivated for a day or two, but it is a bit different story when the journey is one week, one month or even longer. Everybody is different and each person take their motivation in different forms; but the tips I am about to give you are universal, and they will help you to stay motivated, regardless of how long the trip will be for.

First of all, I am not a psychologist, but I have worked with people for many years. I had my own car rental business in Bulgaria, and I still have it today. Now, at the moment, I have a successful business for limousine services, private tours, and airport transfers in Berlin, Germany. I am also an active tour guide and almost every day for the last 20 years, I have spent time talking with different people from around the world. Also, as you already know, I travel a lot with a motorcycle, and over the years, I have seen how different people behave and react in many different situations.

For some people, it's easy to keep doing the same thing, day after day, but for others, this could be a really difficult task. So, how do you do it? How can you stay motivated on a long motorcycle trip?

So, based on everything I have learned, I truly believe that I can give you some useful tips on this topic, and I know that they are going to help you as well.

Let's start it, finally:

Tip number 1: - Choose the right company

This is so important, and if I have to tell you just one tip, then I would pick this. The right friend or friends will give you everything you need to stay motivated, and it doesn't matter how long the trip will be. The right person will help you, inspire you, entertain you, perhaps they may even make you angry from time to time, which could be helpful, sometimes.

To support the last sentence, I will tell you something interesting. I guess that you know Dima. If you don't, he is one of my riding friends. We have taken a number of trips together. He is a great guy and a great rider. When we ride together, we use a Bluetooth system to communicate between ourselves. Usually, we can understand each other perfectly; but on some topics, we have totally different opinions.

Now you are wondering - what topics? Well, the idea of this chapter is to give you some tips, not to tell you what I or Dima believe. Anyway, sometimes when we start arguing on a specific topic, the hours and the km just fly past so quickly, that's why I said that even the disagreements could be helpful.

On the other hand, if you have to ride with the wrong person or group, it is so easy to become demotivated, and to hate every moment of it, even to quit and maybe even to go home.

Some people cannot deal with others. If this is your case, it is better to travel alone. In fact, what I found out is that I feel much better when I am alone. I have no problem with people, and I never had, but on the long trips, I prefer to do it in my own way.

Tip number 2: Set a goal

You need to have a purpose, a goal, or a reason to do it. What exactly this is will really depends on you, but you will need something to keep you motivated all the time. It could be anything: the final destination, meeting with friends, a video or a picture on the specific point, fundraising for a good cause, a self-test or whatever keeps you hooked all the time. The goal will not let you give up, and it will be like your North Star. I promise you that!

Tip number 3: Choose the right motorcycle and the right gear

I have talked a lot about it, and I really hope that you will listen well. Big or small, travel or sports bike, hard or soft luggage, leather or textile…there are so many questions; in fact, you will find so many different opinions for almost any topic you might think about, but in the end, you are the only person who needs to decide. You know yourself, your preferences, and your possibilities. You have to make a choice and live with it later on. The right bike and the right gear will help you to do the trips much safer and easier, on the other hand, if you make the wrong choices, you will remember this for a long time after your trip.

Tip number 4: Take it one day at a time

This way, you don't have to think about how you will make the whole trip, just how to complete the day.

Let me tell you an interesting story:

I was riding with Dima around Pamir Highway in Tajikistan. In our guesthouse, we met a bank manager from Zurich, Switzerland. He was in his late fifties with totally gray hair, traveling by bicycle. His face and hands were quite badly sunburned, it was obvious that he had underestimated the sun. He had been planning this trip for a long time. He wanted to escape the stress of Zurich and travel Pamir by bicycle. He started from Dushanbe about 5 days ago, realizing that it was much more difficult than he imagined. He rode only 250 km and had at least another 1000 more to go. He was totally exhausted, and he decided to quit.

He said:

'I can't do it! These bad roads, the dust, the trucks, the sand…and the heat is just killing me, I won't be able to do it. I give up. Tomorrow I am going home!'

'Wait for a second,' I tried to console him. 'You can always give up and, when you go back, what? I am sure it's not any better at the bank. I am sure that it's another hell altogether, did you forget?'

'I don't know, I didn't expect it to be so hard,' he was shaking his head. 'I won't be able to continue.'

'Look now,' I continued. 'Rest a day or two. Gather your strength, it would be a real pity to give up at this point, you are almost half-way there!'

'Half-way? I am nowhere, my climb hasn't even started yet – no, I won't be able to.' He was stubbornly insisting.

'Listen to what I am going to tell you now,' 'Come with us, we'll have something to eat, and to drink from the magic handmade alcohol we have and we will talk. Tomorrow, if you still feel like it, you can return. In any case, you can't depart now. Each day that you survive here is a great success. It is a defeat that you will always remember when you sit down at your desk at the bank.'

After a couple of hours and a number of drinks he said:

'Man, thank you very much! You convinced me, and I will stay. I will take a day or two off, and then I will continue the trip!'

The same for you, take it one day at a time. This way, you don't have to think about how you will make the whole trip, just how to complete the day.

Tip number 5: - Here, instead of a tip, I have just one question for you: Why do you ride?

And I have some answers ready too:

- **Because this will give me a chance to earn some money from Youtube.**

Be my guest!

- **Because I am looking for an adventure.**

The adventure is a very special state of mind, and it could be reached with almost anything. Walking, running, hiking, swimming, base-jumping, car racing, and more…

- **Because someone said that it is cool!**

You are on the wrong track. Cool for him doesn't mean cool for you.

- **Because I want to see the world**!

That's fine, but are sure that you want to do it with a motorcycle?

- **Because I will be a tough man after that**!

Really? Who said that, your mom?

- **Because I will have these great pictures on Facebook and Instagram**!

If this is the case, then become a photographer, you will succeed much faster.

- **Because all women love adventurers**!

Well…if you haven't experienced love until now, don't expect any changes.

- **Because my kids will be proud of me**!

Could be, but they are more likely to miss you much more than you can imagine.

If you answer is different than these, you actually don't need any motivation! It's simple! Just ride!

*****

How make friends everywhere around the world?

I am glad that you are still here and reading chapter after chapter! This is just a confirmation for me and for you that you really want to go to the next level. One of the most important skills that you will need is the ability to make friends. Without real friends around the world, it will be very hard to achieve the goals you have set.

Some people do it easily, but for some, it is so difficult, do you know why?

Because they just don't know how! This is a skill, one that we usually learn when we are kids. Playing in the kindergarten, school or in the neighborhood. The problem in modern days is that most of the kids never play out. During my childhood, I was spending all of my time out of the home. The worst nightmare I had was my father locking me indoors at home. It was like a death sentence for me. I was sitting at the window all day long, missing the freedom and my friends outside.

With my kids now, it is completely different. The only friends they have are digital. I am not saying that social networks are something bad, no! They could be very useful, especially for this international communication, but in the end, you still need the skills I just mentioned. For that purpose, you need to go out and practice. No other option I'm afraid!

You might say now: Pavlin, it is easy for you, you have a Youtube channel and everybody knows you!

Well, it is true that I have the channel and many people know me, and this definitely helps me to meet many people, but it cannot help me make friends. Also, do not forget that I started working seriously with the channel about three years ago, but I travelled around the world for more than 15 years. Actually, the first time that I left my country for a long period of time was in 1999, which is exactly 20 years ago now. During that period, I met many people, and with some of them, I now have a long term friendship.

So what is the tip, what is the easy way to do it? Actually, there are many tips, and I am going to share them with you right now:

Tip N:1 – Be yourself.

This is so obvious, but many people somehow still manage to miss it. To pretend to be someone else is a common mistake for many. People are not stupid, and if you are not real, then sooner or later, they will understand it. Be yourself, and you will find many people like you. The phrase **'fake it until you make it'** is absolute nonsense for me. Be a real person, and you will meet real friends.

Tip N: 2 – Be careful with religion.

Respect other religions and don't flag with yours. It doesn't matter what you believe, it is a fact that we are all human beings. Do not even think that you or your religion are better than others. This is the fastest way to put yourself in trouble. Some people are very sensitive on that topic and sometimes simple words could be understood incorrectly and create serious problems. It's not worth the risk, and there are plenty of other good things to talk about.

Tip N: 3 – Don't give advice until someone asks for it.

This is exactly what I do at the moment, giving you advice; but keep in mind that the situation is different. I have been on Youtube, Facebook, Instagram, and many more platforms for a long time now. I have proved myself many times, and you already know me. This is actually the reason you are probably reading this book right now. Even so, some of my advice is not going to be for you. I will say that you are not always ready to listen. That's why I will suggest the following:

Save your advice, because people won't listen. You might be right, but they don't care…

When you are trying to give advice to people who are not ready to listen, the chances to hit the wall are very high. Don't do it! Be patient and wait. If someone needs help or advice, you will know about it.

Tip N: 4 – Do not talk, just listen.

I am sure that you have heard the phrase – 'silence is golden'. Most of the people I meet on the road prefer to talk instead of listening. There will be some exceptions, but you will know that anyway. Even if you are coming from a big and powerful country, it doesn't mean that your stories are more interesting. Everybody deserves an audience; so be patient and listen. This will open many unexpected doors for you.

Tip N: 5 – Don't say no if someone offers you a drink.

I am not encouraging you to drink alcohol, but it is a fact that this is the fastest way to break the ice, especially in Russia! Let me tell you one funny story:

A couple of years ago I was in deep Siberia Yakutsk. I was introduced to a couple of local guys and of course, being Russians, they immediately offered me Vodka. I have never been a serious drinker, so I said no. This, of course, unlocked a number of questions:

'Why you don't drink?' – Because I don't want to.

'Ok, but why, do you have health problems?' – No!

'Because of religion？ '– No!

'Your wife did not let you?' – No!

'Are you a spy?' No!

'Are you policeman?' – No!

'Do you plan to ride now?' – No!

After a few more questions, it was my turn to ask, and I said:

'I just don't drink, why are you asking so much?'

And he replied: 'Because here in Russia, we don't have people like you!'

After that, he stopped asking, but somehow the conversation was going nowhere. He was trying to ask something, but he cannot, in the end I said to him:

'Listen, I understand that it is very difficult for you to talk without drinking, so please give me one glass and let's start again!'

Guess what, the conversation continued until 4 a.m., and today, we are still friends after more than 15 years.

There are some exceptions around the world, like Mongolia, where I was advised by the Russians never to drink with the locals, but as I said, there are just a few exceptions.

Tip N: 6 - Always stop if you see a broken down car or motorcycle.

Sometimes, just a simple gesture can make a big difference. Do not be afraid to talk with unknown people, especially if you see that they need help. There are a few situations like this that actually resulted in great long-term friendships with people.

I had a funny situation in Pakistan. We were on the top of Babusar Pass when we saw a couple of local guys shaking their heads around one bike. When we got closer, we saw that they couldn't start the engine because the owner lost the key. I knew how to start the bike without the key. It took me just a couple of minutes to fix their problem by cutting the cables and adding it together to simulate the job of the key. I was doing what I had to do, and my friend Anif was translating:

'Have you seen the red light now – No, what about now, yes it came. Okay, put it in neutral – ok, it is done. Kick the starter now…'

The guy kicked the pedal, the engine started, and they said all together at the same time, 'Mashhalah'! Then I had to explain to them what to do when they got home. One of the guys was talking in really good English, and he was very grateful and actually invited us to his home. At that moment, we didn't need this help, but it was there simply because of the simple act of humanity.

Tip N: 7 – Talk with locals.

See what they like and say some good words about it. You don't need to lie, just be honest. Another example is from Turkmenistan. I stopped in a local restaurant, and because it was in the afternoon, there was no one there; just me, Dima, and the owner. The place has just had a renovation and was looking very good. I said this to the owner and asked him a couple of questions about the details, and we had a great conversation. Just before we left, he asked us where we staying and invited us to his home. At the time we said no, because we had already booked a hotel, but because of the unexpected circumstances, we needed to stay one more day and guess where we were? We also had very nice company with the whole family. Great people, I will never forget them!

Tip N: 8 – Do not forget to be thankful for the food.

In some countries around the world, people don't have your possibilities. It might be difficult for them to serve you even a normal dinner. Be grateful, and always say thank you! Especially to the women. Most of the time, they live in the shadows of their husbands and when you like the food they prepare, you will be always welcome in their home.

Tip N: 9 – Bring some small gifts.

Could be anything. A souvenir from your country or anything you may choose. But it is very important to give something. The price of it doesn't matter, but it will make a huge difference in your relations.

Tip N: 10 – You cannot say Thank you enough!

By saying this, I mean that you have to say thank you for everything! Even if the person on the other side said that you don't have to thank them all the time, just do it! Believe it or not, this will push the person to make even more of an effort for you, because this is how humans react. This is a proven fact! You can even try it with your wife!

Once again, these tips have helped me over the last 20 years to travel to so many places trouble-free and to make many friends! I hope you enjoy them.

*****

Tips to Avoid Motorcycle Accidents

To have an accident is the worst nightmare for any motorcycle rider, isn't it? Before I even start with the tips, I want to tell you something very important. It is something that you have to keep in mind every time when you start up your motorcycle. I know that you might disagree with what I am about to tell you, but I hope that at least one small part will stick in your mind, and it will be like a seed for your future thoughts in this direction!

Are you ready to listen? Not only to read it, are you ready to actually listen? If not, please go and find something else, because this is the most important piece of advice I can give you!

'Every accident you already had, or you might have in the future was and will be your fault!'

I know that it is hard to swallow the truth, but think twice, replay the situations or the accidents you have had in your mind, and you will see the mistakes you have made and the possible future ways to avoid it.

Of course, as I said at the beginning, I do not expect from everyone to agree with this statement. You might have some arguments:

You are not right, the car hit me from behind, the truck came from my left or in this situation I had the right of way or many more…

Yes, the car hit you from behind, but did you check the mirrors properly before that?

The truck came from the left, ok, but how the hell did you miss the whole truck coming from the left, where was your attention?

I had the right of way, all right, but it means nothing when somebody takes it from you, does it?

All of these excuses or possible situations might help with the insurance policy, but not with the pain and the shame after that!

I will start with one personal story. It is a bit long, but please be patient; in the end, you will get the point.

In 2001, I was in Germany. At that time, Bulgaria was not part of the European Union, and with my driver license, I was able to drive a car or ride a motorcycle for 6 months. After that, I needed to get a German license, but not only to change it, like today; I had to do the whole test, both the theoretical and the practical.

One day, exactly one week after the 6 months period expired, I was driving my car in Munich, 600km away from Berlin, where I was living at that time. A Policeman stopped me on the road and asked for my license. After a couple of minutes, he said:

'Ooooo, you don't have a license!'

I tried to explain that I had, and it is only one week since the period expired and if he let me go I will drive straight to Berlin and get my license sorted; but… as you know what Germans are like, he said:

'I cannot do this sir! I cannot allow you to drive without a license!'

He also locked my car, took my documents, and let me know that he will only give it back to a person with a valid driver license. So, I had to call a friend to come, and so on, and so on. Just to make the long story short, after that I had to go through the whole procedure which I had already done when I was 18 years old, just to have a new license.

During that time, I found out something very interesting with the German test. It was a short sentence saying, that **when you drive your car or motorcycle, you have to predict the mistakes of others.** I had never heard this before, even though I had my license from a long time ago. This is actually my first tip for you:

N: 1 – Predict the mistakes of others

Which means to ride at the speed which will allow you to predict the mistakes of other drivers or riders and prevent any possible accidents.

You cannot do anything if you are filtering with 100km per hour between the lines and somebody opens a door unexpectedly, but it will be a different story if you ride at 30 and you are ready to brake at any time. It is the same with overtakes, stops, acceleration, and everything else related to motorcycle riding.

In fact, during my last trip to Pakistan, India, Nepal, and Bangladesh, I realized why they don't have so many accidents, even though it was the worst traffic I have ever seen, because they just follow this rule: '**Predict the mistake of others!**'

N: 2 – Choose the proper bike.

In the last two years, I have talked a lot on that topic. In fact, in my first book, I have a number of chapters; what bike, how to choose the bike, and many more. I will summarise it for you and will say that a 1000cc sports bike shouldn't be your first motorcycle, especially if you are 18 years old. A KTM 1290 Adventure is not the right choice if you are 170cm. A Harley Davidson cannot be ridden off-road, and it is no fun at all to ride a 150cc bike on the highways.

By choosing the right model for you and your riding style, you will actually minimize the risk to have an accident by more than 50%. You have to be able to control your motorcycle alone, without any help.

Nowadays, everybody is obsessed with these big engines, more power, more top speed, and expensive adventure gadgets; but not so many people make the most practical choice and buy the bike they really need.

N: 3 – Know your limits

The first thing you have to do is to learn how to ride. With this, I don't mean to start the engine, go to the next traffic light, make a u-turn, twist the throttle on the straight line, make some tilts, avoid some obstacles, and make an emergency stop!

No! These techniques you have to learn to get a driver license. I mean to learn how to ride your motorcycle in any situation: Good or bad weather, cold or extreme heat, summer or winter conditions, asphalt, dirt roads, gravel, sand, mud or any other type of terrain you find.

When you complete this first step, you will gain some important skills. For example, you will know how dangerous it is to ride in the winter, how risky it is to chop the throttle on the sand or how stupid it is to press the front brake on the corners and many more... You will know your limits, and this will help you to avoid unnecessary accidents.

N: 4 – Be informed

Let me clarify this point for you; Most of the accidents will happen when we venture into unknown territory. It could be a new city, different traffic rules, bad roads or unexpected weather changes.

You can minimize the risks if you just do your homework. Read as much information as possible about the place that you are going to visit. Ask people, read books, watch videos, be ready or at least be informed about what you are going to face.

After I uploaded the last episodes in Ladakh, India I have received many comments from people asking me was I not afraid to go there; it looked so dangerous and many more…

Here, I have to remind you again about the previous tip, **Know your limits**.

Do not even think that because I have this Youtube channel or I have been to a few places around the world that I consider myself as a great rider! No! Absolutely no, but I ride motorcycles for many years, and I know my limits.

I know where, what bike, in what terrain, and how long I can ride for. Before the trip, and even during the trip, I was constantly upgrading my information about Ladakh, checking the weather conditions and the roads, so finally when I reached the destination, I was sure that I could make it.

Of course, there is always a 10% unpredicted risk, but I accept that, because if everything is 100% secure, where is the adventure?

N: 5 – *Fear is better than gear*

Sounds good, doesn't it? Sometimes, I have these great ideas! What do I mean by saying that? With the word **gear,** I mean everything that you need to travel – motorcycle, helmet, jacket, boots, and all of the adventure stuff you have already bought.

- Even the best helmet cannot guarantee 100% safety!

- Instead of relying on your ABS, learn how to stop properly!

- The tires keep the bike on the ground, but not always, not in any case!

- Auxiliary lights cannot guarantee that you will be visible; sometimes people miss even a 20 ton truck with 20 lights on the top!

- By buying an expensive motorcycle, you are not going to be a better rider, just an owner of a more expensive motorcycle!

- Traction control is a great extra, but only sometimes!

- The crash bars might protect your motorcycle, but not you!

- All the additional features you might have on the bike cannot help you ride it, you have to do it!

- Nothing is worth more than your life!
-

Please read this chapter at least twice! I really hope that you will remember it!

*****

How to get maximum fuel efficiency?

Did you ever ask yourself why motorcycles use so much petrol? I guess not, but would you like to learn how to save some money on fuel? In this chapter, I will give you 10 proven tips on how to get the maximum fuel efficiency from any motorcycle; keep reading!

As you know, everybody tries to save money one way or another. I personally believe that the money spent on petrol to travel around the world is maybe one of the best investments, but it doesn't mean that I am happy to pay more than I should.

I will repeat the question from the beginning;

'Did you ever ask yourself why motorcycles use so much petrol?'

I mean, why is it that motorcycles use about the same amount of petrol as a normal-sized car?

Let's take an average car, like a VW Polo; It is 1,350kg and uses around 4.8 – 5l per 100km. Fair enough, but one motorcycle, like my Yamaha, for example, is about 200kg and uses 4.5-5l per 100km, why? Even with me on the top, I am 100kg + 200 for the bike, it's 300kg all together, it is still 4 times lighter, so why?

It is because of the aerodynamic shape. If you just do some simple research on the internet, you will find a lot of pictures of cars in a wind tunnel. You can see how the wind goes over the top of the car very smoothly, and the better the shape, the faster the car will go and the less petrol it will use.

You can also find pictures about how a motorcycle performs in a wind tunnel. It will become immediately clear that any motorcycle has a terrible aerodynamic shape.

So, because of the shape of the motorcycle, this is essentially why they use so much petrol.

'Pavlin, wait a second, this is clear physics, I know this already, but how will this help me with the fuel efficiency?'

Well, this question actually leads me to the tips I promised to give you.

N: 1 – Try to improve your aerodynamic shape.

If you just stand in front or behind a motorcycle with hard cases, you will see how wide they are. Actually the bike will be like a sail, creating this constant stopping power and of course, raise the fuel consumption by at least half liter per 100km. This is what I noticed with very light saddle bags. With big and square hard cases it will be even worse. Install a windscreen if you don't have one already. It will improve efficiency and also help you with any fatigue.

N: 2 – Constant instead of top speed.

This will help you more than you can even imagine. There is no way you can ride at 160km on the highways and expect your fuel consumption to be efficient, no way. The best way to know what the most efficient speed on your motorcycle will be is to keep the RPM in the middle of the scale. For example, if the max is 8000, keep in the 4000 - 4,500 range, and you will be ok. We have a word in Bulgaria about it, and I am not so sure that I can translate it correctly, but will be something like:

'The running horses always eat more!'

N. 3 – Quality petrol.

Always try to use the best quality of petrol you can find at the moment. I know that in some countries this is very difficult, but you can bring some octane boosters with you and still have what you need. Even if you pay more for it in the end, you will save money in the long run.

N: 4 – Proper maintenance

A new air filter, new spark, and ignition coil will significantly improve the work of the engine, which of course, will reduce the overall fuel consumption.

N: 5 – Be gentle with the throttle.

With this, I am not saying that you have to ride at 30km per hour, no; but you don't need to be the first on every traffic light. Try to avoid nonsense accelerations, because they usually lead to hard braking and new acceleration after that. Be gentle, and you will notice the difference next time when you need to refill the tank.

N: 6 – Turn off the engine

If you need to wait for more than a minute, for example on the red light, construction works or traffic jam, always turn off the engine. The reason I say more than a minute is because with every start and stop you shorten the life of the battery, starter, oil, and even the engine. Yes, you will save some money on petrol, but then you will spend it for something else. This is why I don't really like this stop and go option in modern cars.

N: 7 - Tire pressure.

Flat or not properly inflated tires could raise fuel consumption more than you can imagine. Check what your manual says and always check the pressure before you go. Knobby tires will always use a bit more petrol.

N: 8 – Use the correct gear.

Almost every rider will advise you to go to a higher gear as fast as possible with the idea to save fuel, but I cannot really agree with this statement. I don't think that riding with 20km per hour in 6th gear, even if the bike allows you to do so, will help with fuel efficiency. Choose the proper gear for every situation. For example, if you go downhill, the bike uses less petrol when you keep it in gear without throttle, than idling on neutral. Going uphill in 6th gear, when you should be using 4th is not going to help you at all.

N: 9 – Always start in the cold mornings

I know that this is not always possible, but if you can, then you should do it. If you have the chance to start early morning, when usually the temperature is 5 to 10 degrees colder, then the engine will work much better than in the hotter part of the day. The reason for that is because when the air is cold it shrinks, and actually the engine will receive more air for the same amount of time. This will increase the power and of course, will lead to the desired petrol efficiency. This is actually what an intercooler in vehicles does; it cools down the air before it gets into the engine.

N: 10 – Be smart

With this, I meant that you have to be ready with solutions for every possible problem and situations. For example, if you know that in the next 300km you will cross the area with expensive petrol, full the tank before that. In many countries around the world, including Germany the petrol prices are different in the nights and days. Always use the lower price and you will be surprised from the monthly results.

All right, these were the tips I wanted to tell you, and they are universal for any bike. Now I want to tell you something about the difference between some of the systems, and why one is better than another.

N: 1 – Injection is always better

I know that there are so many riders who love their carburetors, but they have to confess that the fuel injections are far more economical than any carburetor. They are designed to provide the best fuel efficiency at any given moment. It doesn't matter how hot or cold it is, what the elevation is or what mechanic skills the rider has. Yes, I will agree, that if you know how to adjust the carburetor you might get even better results, but do you have these skills?

N: 2 – Forget about the air-cooled engines

Yes, correct, forget about it! It is more and more difficult to find, and they will completely disappear in a couple of years. The reason for that is because they are old and inefficient technology. To provide the best results, the engine needs to keep at the same temperature, at either 90 or 95 degrees; that's why with water-cooled engines we have thermostats, to keep this correct. With the air-cooled engines, this temperature moves all the time. Cold on the highways, hot in the traffic or even too much when we stay still. All of these wear the engine much faster and of course cannot guarantee the same fuel efficiency.

So next time when you are looking for a new bike, just keep this in mind!

*****

Ferries, visas, temporary import and carnet de passage

If you don't have any plans to ride your motorcycle abroad, then this information is not for you. However, if you are born with a spirit of adventure, like me, then keep reading, because I will tell you the most important things about ferries, Visas, Temporary import and carnet de passage.

I was lucky to be born in Europe and to be able to travel to so many countries without even needing to cross any borders. That was great, but sooner or later, even Europe become small and I start to look for different routes. Of course, some of them required all of the things I already mentioned. I know that for you, this might sound like an impossible mission, but actually, it's not that bad as long as you know what you are doing. Read it carefully until the end, because all the information I will share with you will help you out and save you many problems and money in the future.

Ferries

As I said, I live in Europe, but you might be from the UK, USA, Africa or even Australia. So if you want to see the world, you need to ship your bike. Ferries are maybe the best option at the moment. The procedure is very easy. What you need to do is just to go online and book your ticket. The companies, the ferry lines, and the prices will depend on your country. You can easily find it on Google.

To get on the boat is also easy, just make sure that you are on time at the port and there will be more than enough people to tell you what to do and where to go. The best option is usually when you book an overnight ferry, so you actually don't need to worry about the hotel. For long distances, like the USA or Australia, it is always worth to check the prices for shipping your bike by plane. In many cases, it could be cheaper and much faster.

Tips for ferries:

- Lock all the stuff you don't need on the bike. Helmet, jacket, pants, boots...
- Make sure that your lights and GPS are off.
- Do not forget the key in the ignition.
- Bring some soft cushions to add under the belts, especially if you have an expensive bike.
- The side stand is usually more stable than a centre stand.

Visas

Here we come to a more difficult situation. If you live in a big capital city, most of the embassies will be there, but if you are, somewhere in the country, you will probably need to travel. Also, keep in mind that you need to make the trip twice, once to apply for a visa and once to receive it. In some embassies, they might have an option to send your passport back. Many countries also offer an online Visa service, but in most cases, you need to send the passport to the embassy to actually add your Visa in. I know that this sounds very discouraging, but when you make it once, everything else will be much easier.

So, a few pieces of advice before you go to the embassy:

- You need an international passport.
- Your passport needs to be valid for a 6 month period from the date you intend to leave.
- You should have enough blank pages for your visas.
- Make sure that you have enough money to pay the fees. In 90% of cases, they will only accept card payments or a wire transfer in advance. The information about the price and the bank details can be found on their websites. Note: Paying the fees does not guarantee your visa.
- Check the working hours of the embassy. Most of them are open for just a couple of hours per day. Make sure that you know when. You don't want to travel 200km and find out that they are closed.
- Read about the documents they require in advance by visiting their website. In every country, the requirements are different. Some might want an invitation, travel insurance or some might need to see your bank statement to prove that you have enough money to travel. In many cases, you need to book hotels or flight tickets in advance. If you need to do it, make sure that

you did it with the option to cancel it after that. First, because they might not give you the Visa, and the second is because the plan might change.
- Print the application and fill it before you go there. You don't need to complete it in a hurry when you are at the embassy when you are surrounded by many people. Do it at home. Most of the embassies have the form ready for downloading from their websites.
- Make a photocopy of all of the documents and keep them handy just in case they ask for it.
-

How to behave once you get there?

This sounds like a stupid question, but believe me, it is not. Show some respect, dress well and shave your face if necessary. Do not go dressed in shorts and thongs. Even in the summer, you should wear long pants and a shirt. You might think that this doesn't matter because you are American, German or whatever type of citizen you are, (nothing personal, just an example), but actually, it always matters. Some of the people behind the desks spend their entire life talking with people like you. Believe or not, they have the power to refuse or at least to slow down your application if they decide to.

Do not be arrogant and show some respect. Always wait if they ask you something and never say bad things about their country. It should be the opposite. Tell them how great their country is, and how beautiful it is, how you cannot wait to get there and many more things like this. These nice words, combined with your honest smile will open all the doors for you.

The example I can give you now is from my last Indian Visa. I filled the application online, but I could not print it. I don't know why something went wrong. I tried a couple of times, but I couldn't, so finally, I just printed the application number and my name and went into the embassy. So, I was waiting for my number to come and even though there was no one there I was waiting for the guy behind the desk to tell me that I can step in. He asked a few standard questions, where did I want to go, and what was the purpose of my visit; I explained everything to him in great detail. I told him that I wanted to visit India ever since I was a child, and my mother was reading me about these great Indian stories. Which is true by the way, and he was listening with a smile on his face. I explained to him about the situation in Iran and so on. So, actually, we chatted for about 3-5 min before he even looked at my documents. After that, he saw that my form was not printed and my picture was not exactly the size they needed, but he said:

'I will print it for you, and I will not send you back for another picture because you are a nice man!'

So, all of this cost me nothing, it was even a pleasure to talk with this guy.

One very important thing to consider is the time that you will need to receive the visa. Usually, it can be anything from one to four weeks. Which means that your passport will stay there and you cannot go to another embassy until you get it back. Keep that in mind, especially if you need to make a couple of Visas. Make sure that you have enough time.

Temporary import.

As I said in Europe, you don't need to worry about it; but outside of Europe, you will definitely need it. This is basically a declaration which you have to fill at the border. It will be given to you by the border officers, and you need to complete it there. It is nothing special: Your name, nationality, passport number, then your bike make, model, engine size, VIN, and registration plate numbers. The dates you are entering, the border name, and many more details just like this. Usually, they have it in a few languages, not everywhere, but at least at most of the borders. You can always ask for help from somebody with more experience around you. You have to fill in two copies, sign it, and then go to the counter.

Once that is fone, you just need to wait for it to be stamped, and signed from the border officers. You will receive one of the copies which one you have to keep until you leave the country. This is a very important document. Make sure that you have it in a very safe place. If the police stop you somewhere around the country, they will probably want to see it. Also, do not forget to bring a pen.

Important:

The Visa and temporary import are two different things. The visa is for you as a person, and the document is for your vehicle or motorcycle.

Carnet de Passage

This is perhaps the most difficult procedure or at least the most expensive. This is very similar to the temporary import declaration, but in this case, your country guarantees that the bike will not be sold there. The difference is, that instead of filling these pages you will have it already prepared in a folder. The number of the pages depends on the number of countries you want to visit. One page is for one country, but if you get out and you need to come in again, like me from India to Nepal and back to India, this means that you need two pages only for India. It is the same if you plan to use the same route on the way back home. One country, one entry, one page. This actually is much easier than to fill in the declarations on the border, but it comes at a price. It is different in every country, but they all charge for the number of the pages you need. It is not so bad, but you need also to pay a deposit. This is also dependant on the country and on the price of your motorcycle. The deposit will be returned to you once you return back home with your motorcycle. The problem is, that if you have an expensive bike, you have to be ready to hand over at least a 5,000 euro deposit for just a couple of months, and not everyone can afford this. You can also have this carnet on the border, but it will cost you much more.

You can find an internet list with the different countries that need a carnet de passage at the moment. This document can usually be received in your local automobile club, just google it.

Something very important:

Even if you have a carnet de passage, there is no guarantee that you will be able to visit the country. It is just a document for your vehicle, nothing more!

I hope that this information will be useful to you!

*****

How to ride a motorcycle in a foreign country?

To travel to a different country is a bit scary, isn't it? Some people are even worried about leaving their hometown. To step into the unknown, to a completely unknown place sounds like an impossible mission for many of you. Actually, there is nothing to be afraid of, just as long as you follow some simple rules.

1. Respect the religion.

Before I tell you the tip, I would like to tell about one e-mail I have received recently. A subscriber from my channel asked me this:

'I have a big tattoo of a Christian cross on my arm. Do you think that this could be a problem if I plan to travel to a Muslim country?'

This was actually a very good question, and it provoked me to talk about it.

Religion has always been a very sensitive topic. Over the years, millions of people have lost their lives because of the differences in religion they each have. Even today, exactly in this very moment, in many places around the world, people kill each other because of that. The news makes it even worse. If you believe everything you see on the TV, you will come to some very wrong conclusions.

I have one personal story to tell you. I am afraid that it is a bit long, but please be patient, because it will answer many of your future questions.

Maybe you are aware of our history; Bulgaria was, at one time, part of the Ottoman Empire for five centuries, from the 14th to the 19th Centuries. We had learned all of this in school, our parents had told us tales about it, and we had watched many movies about it. Massacres, killings, rape, a time of brutal separations, blood, tax and so forth were the images in my head. Without even realizing it, by the time I was 15 years old, I felt a deep hatred towards Turks and Muslims.

The environment I lived in contributed to my ignorance. I grew up in a small, isolated suburb where everybody knew everybody else. From my teenage years, I had to learn to fight for my place, safeguard my honor and never betray my friends. Very rarely did children from other suburbs come over, but if they did by accident, they would receive a beating and quickly return to where they came from. There was absolutely no presence of Ethnic Turks or people of a Roma descent. Or even if there were, they were single cases and we hadn't noticed. We had always discussed them and shared our common hatred towards those two groups.

The Renaissance process we underwent in 1986 helped a lot in further deepening this created notion of hatred. We had transformed into young patriots or, as I can say now, idiots. The year 1987 marked the creation of new army bases. The general idea was that in all regions with concentrated populations of Muslims, there had to be an army base positioned with at least 300 strong young men ready who were to control and prevent the creation of ethnic unrest by any means necessary. I was sent to one of these so-called bases to complete two years national service. I will not go into detail of my time there, but I will say that by the end of my service, I was ready to do anything they ordered me to. They were able to very skilfully, manipulate my patriotism. I am tremendously grateful I never got to actually put into practice what I had been trained to do. After I completed my service, it took more than fifteen years and numerous contacts with Muslims all over the world to be able to fully comprehend they are just people like all of us.

The moral of that story is that everybody could be very easily brainwashed, but also that anybody can manage to change the way he or she sees the word. Remember it!

So to answer the question about the cross on the arm:

How are you going to feel if the person you talk with has Islamic tattoo on his hand?

Answer this yourself, but be honest!

So, my advice will be: Respect the religion of others and do not flag with yours. Your God might be the best for you, but it is not the same everywhere. Some people are very sensitive on that topic, and you don't need to provoke them even more.

2. Try to give instead of taking.

Be patient. Some people will be very curious to see you and talk to you. They will have hundreds of questions because they don't see riders every day. Give them some simple gifts, tell them some stories and all the doors will be open for you. Once you step into their homes, it will be like one totally different world for you. For one single night, you will learn more than a year of research on the internet.

3. People are the same everywhere

Do not pretend to be different, because you are not. You are human being with a head, body, arms, and legs like anyone else. Try to behave like a normal, respectful person and not like a king of the world. Do not try to teach or change them. Some things cannot be changed. You are not a famous guru, you are just the guy with a motorcycle. You are a guest, so be the guest you would like to meet at your home. Choose your words carefully and learn how to listen.

4. Don't argue or drink with locals.

You can do it only if you have friends there. This is very important! If a friend offers you a drink, it is always better to take it, but not with unknown people.

As you probably know, alcohol can transform anyone from a normal person into a real devil. When you mix it with some bad words, it could become a real problem. Do not even think that you can fight with a couple of people because you are a strong man. You cannot! I have tried this few times in my life and … then I realized that it's not like in Hollywood. The result will be a shame and a lot of pain!

5. Obey the rules.

If you don't know the rules of the country, then you need to find them out and make sure that you do not break them. Do not argue with the Police and don't be arrogant. Believe me, they have seen many like you before and this not going to help you at all. Calm down, confess your mistakes, and ask for a compromise. In most of the countries around the world, the police are tolerant with motorcycle riders, just be patient and you will be fine.

6. Always carry a paper map.

I don't have to explain to you how useful a map is. A map will give you the chance to talk with the locals, and ask for directions. They might even be able to suggest some nice routes for you. Yes, yes, you can do it on your phone or GPS, but try it with some old guy in the middle of nowhere and then we will talk again. The map will be interesting for them as well. They will want to see it and show you some really nice places. The information they can give you is priceless!

7. Water & food.

Do not drink water from the rivers, lakes or even the pipe system before you are absolutely sure that it's ok to do so. Again, ask the locals. This could save you a lot of problems and some serious diseases. Be careful with food as well. I know that many of you will love to test some local drinks or meals, but keep in mind that the taste could be totally different from what you know.

8. Petrol

In some countries, the petrol stations will be different than the ones you know. Be ready to have some really low-quality petrol. If your bike requires premium petrol only, then make sure that you have some octane boosters or additives ready to use.

9. Always keep cash

Always keep cash in the local currency. Credit cards mean nothing in some countries, they are just a useless piece of plastic. Cash could save you a lot of problems. Of course, never show your money in public places.

10. Always take your rubbish with you.

I know that it is very easy to forget this when you are not at home, but this is a home for someone and you have to respect that! It will cost you nothing, but it will be a good example for many after you. Especially if you have the chance to share this on Facebook, Youtube or whatever social network you use.

I hope this information will give you some courage and push you to your desired destination even quicker.

*****

How to make the right decisions?

Our life is the result of all the choices we have made in the past, and the future is in our hands! In this chapter, I will tell you 5 easy ways to make the right decisions, regardless of the situation you are in at the moment.

Making the right decisions has never been easy. The harder the situation is, the more difficult the choices are. So what is the trick? What is the easy way to deal with this problem? I will tell you, don't even worry about it, but before I open the magic box, I have to prepare you for the contents that are inside.

As usual, I will start with my philosophical thoughts and some personal examples, but this is the only way I know. It is easy to say something quickly, but what is the point if you cannot get it. I am sure that you have had teachers like this in your childhood. They were like machine guns that just replayed that boring history or whatever they were teaching with the idea that we are going to learn it! No way!

Our brains are very powerful biological computers, but even so, they need some data to work better and to understand more easily, and this what I am giving you now.

The first thing you have to remember is:

'There are no problems, only solutions!'

For every possible problem, you will find at least 3 solutions. Okay, but how do you know which one is right?

To tell you what I mean by this, I have to tell you a personal story. I had a flat tire in Ladakh (North India) at about 5000m above the sea level. The problem was, that I did not have a pump or air compressor with me, I had only 3 CO containers.

Instead of fixing or changing the tire, because I had a spare tube with me, I decided to ride until I finished the containers and then even more 50km with a completely flat tire.

Of course, I have everything on video which I uploaded to Youtube with the title 'Did I make a mistake on that day?'

Actually, I made it on purpose. Because I already had an idea to talk about it, but I needed some information. I needed to know how people will react. I needed their answers.

Wow, I just confessed that I used the viewers for my social experiment! Shame on me!

Yes, I did it, because everything I learned actually helped me to make my conclusions and structure my thoughts, which I believe will help you to learn how to make the right decisions!

So, about 99% of the people replied that it was an obvious mistake. They said that I should have changed the tire when I had the chance, or that I should have had an air pump or compressor with me, and many other suggestions.

It was obvious that I made a mistake. Not only one, actually two mistakes:

I shouldn't have gone alone, and I should have had an air compressor with me. These were the mistakes I have made, but, here you go, the important BUT again! These were the mistakes that I made before the situation with the flat tire, not as a result of it.

I was alone many days before and after that. I did not have a pump or air compressor in Pakistan or throughout the entirety of my trip through India. I bought one in Delhi afterwards.

Yes, I learned my lessons and even made a detailed video about it, and I hope that many will watch it before they decide to go to Ladakh.

Here you might get a bit confused and even ask:

'So, what happened on that day? Was it a mistake or not?'

Be patient my friend, the learning process is never easy…let's finally, start with the tips:

N: 1 – See the whole picture

Instead of focusing exactly on the point, or on the problem you have at the moment, try to see the whole picture.

With the story that I just told you everyone was focused on the problem they saw at the moment which was the flat tire. All the advice or the suggestions were what I should have done or what I had to do, but none of you, no actually, only one person replied differently. Let me explain to you with more detail:

They focused on the flat tire, but by doing it, so they have missed the whole picture. Let's see it again:

Problem – Flat tire. Possible solutions:

1. Use patches.
2. Change the tube.
3. Ride and go down as fast as possible.

99% chose option number one or two. I chose option 3; why? Because I looked at the whole picture and this is how it was looking at me:

Problem – flat tire. Location **Ladakh**. Have you seen that I even bolded the name Ladakh? If this still means nothing to you, then keep reading:

Location of the problem Ladakh! Full picture:

Elevation: almost 5,000m.

Time: 2 p.m.

No telephone or internet signal.

At the end of the season (unpredictable weather).

No traffic: (4 trucks for the whole day).

Temperature: around zero.

Nearest village: about 70km.

Now, after I showed you the whole picture, let's see the options again:

1. Use patches. They cannot really work well, because of the cold weather.

2. Change the tube.

There were a number of times that I have had flat tires on my bikes, and every time, there was no problem to fix it. To use patches or a new tube, whatever was better at the moment. However, once I had a flat somewhere around North Germany, and the tire was Metzeler Karoo. I opened it easily and changed the tube, but I could not mount it again. After more than 2 hours of battling, I gave up and left the bike on the road. Thankfully it was in Germany, and I was able to walk with the wheel to the first village. From there, I took a taxi to the local garage and they fixed it. The guy from the tire service said that this was the most difficult tire to mount that he had ever seen. All of this happened in the summer, I was very close to the village, and it was at sea- level.

With this in mind, I look again at the current situation:

Elevation almost 5,000m. **Difficult to breathe, which meant it was hard to get out and put the tire on again.**

Time: 2 p.m. **No time for mistakes.**

No telephone or internet signal. **Cannot call a friend.**

At the end of the season (unpredictable weather). **Possible weather change.**

No traffic (4 trucks for the whole day). **Very low chances of finding help.**

Temperature: around zero. **Cold rubber and cold metal, both equal to harder work, which means a possible failure.**

Nearest village: about 70km. **Not walking distance. I cannot spend the night there.**

With all of these in my mind, I had only one solution:

3. Ride and go down as fast as possible.

I did it, and I reached the point I needed. On the next day, I was able to ride again and even to leave the mountain in the last possible moment. After me, they actually closed the Rothang pass, because of the bad weather.

Even if I had a compressor, I would have probably taken the same decision. The only difference will be that I would not have needed to ride with a flat tire.

You have to learn to see the whole picture with every problem in your life.

N: 2 – Think out of the box

I would say that because I am coming from East Europe, for me, or many people like me this is an easy job. Because the life we have had in the past, and it never being as safe and secure as most of the western countries, we were always ready with some easy solutions or out of the box thinking.

Here, I will give you another example with my riding friend Dima.

In 2016, we were riding in Morocco. Exactly on my birthday, he fell down and broke his leg. It was obvious that for him the trip was over, but we still have a problem with the bike. Because it was with temporary import declaration, he was unable to leave the country without it, but the problem was, that we were 1000km away from the Spanish border

The possible options were to load the bike and Dima into a van or truck and go to the border. Yes, but no! There are no vans for rent in Morocco, and the only transportation company we found was asking for 1,500$. Regardless of the advice or the suggestions we have, Dima said: I will ride it, and he did it. He rode the bike 1000km with a broken leg. At the end, we all confessed that this was the best decision, even though it was not logical at all.

So think out of the box and be creative.

N: 3 – Trust your sixth sense.

Again, I have to give you an example from my last trip. Right after the day with the flight tire, I spent the night in Keylong. On the next day, I was able to buy the last possible tire in the town and immediately go to Rohtang pass. Even though some local riders suggested that it was best to stay, because the weather was changing very fast. I just listened to my sixth sense and went through. Yes, it was hard, but I managed to go safely.

A couple of hours after me, they closed the pass. For how long I have no idea, but once the winter starts there, you never know how long it will take.

Always trust your sixth sense, the internal voice, God, or whatever you want to name it.

N: 4 – Always put others' needs before your own

By saying this, I mean to respect your riding friends, yours and their machines as well. Every decision needs to be taken with this in mind. Sometimes it is easy to say 'yes' or 'No,' but it will be difficult to live with the consequences after that.

Yes, it will be easy to call a friend to save your ass in the middle of the night, because you forgot to put petrol or because the bike breaks down, but did you considered that he needs to drive all night long just to come here?

If you asked your friend to pull your bike for 100km because you burned your clutch did you have in mind that this might burn his clutch as well?

Even if they insist on helping you or doing something for you, always think twice!

Respect your friends and their machines.

N: 5 – Think with a long perspective

All the decisions need to be taken with a long perspective. Do not go on a risky off-road track if you still have so many km ahead. The trip is more important than a moment of fun.

The example I can give you now is from Morocco. One of the days we were in Merzouga, the hotel was right in the middle of a desert. One of the local guys offered us a unique journey through the desert. 350km of pure adventure, no roads, no people, nothing. They offered us an assistance car, a 4x4 to guide us, so we can unload the bikes and enjoy the ride. So far so good, but the price they asked was 600 Dollars. We were altogether 4 people. If we split the cost it will be 150 per person, the problem was that two of the guys immediately said – no, so we need to pay 300 Dollars each.

It was too much for a one day ride because with this money we would be able to ride for one week or even more in Morocco, so I said No.

My friend really wanted to do it, even though he didn't have very much off-road experience, but he just wanted it and tried to convince me to go without assistance.

He said: It will be a nice adventure, we can make it and many more words like this…

Here, I am sure that knowing me, you thought that I did it, but no, I did not. What I said to him was:

'Listen my friend: To ride in the desert, without assistance on a road we don't know with these heavy bikes, and all of our luggage is a big challenge. I can try it for 50 or maybe 100km, but 350 is just too much. I won't take the risk. We haven't completed Morocco, and after that, we still need to ride 4,000km to Germany. I am not going to risk the entire trip for one day of fun in the desert!'

You have to prioritize your trips. To know what is most important and always think with a long perspective.

*****

Tips for Solo Riders

Are you ready to travel alone? Are you ready to test your real adventure spirit? I guess yes, or at least you have plans to do it. Not everybody is ready to make this step, but I can guarantee that if you do it once you will do it again and again. In the end, you will realize that the pros are much more than cons.

Of course, as usual, I don't expect from you to agree with me just like that, but that's okay. I am not here to argue with you or to prove my theory. I just want to share what I have learned after many km of solo riding with the idea to help.

Like most of the things we are afraid of, it looks so scary when you know nothing about it. Most of the people believe that traveling with a group is much safer. It could be, but it could be also the other way around. I already told you a couple of times that safety is just an illusion. With the decisions that we take in any given moment, we actually maximize or minimize the risk to have an accident or even to die.

Nothing and no one cannot guarantee 100% safety! Remember it!

All right, that's enough on the topic of riding alone or in a group. Now, as I promised at the beginning, I will give you 10 proven tips for solo riding.

Listen carefully, and I guarantee that they will bring you only positives.

Tip N: 1 – You need a goal

Having a good purpose for the trip is the best advice I can give you. I am not saying that the rest of the trips will be crap, no, but they will be more to the technical part of the journey. Having a great purpose or goal will be more like the soul of the trip. This is the thing that will push you to keep riding day after day, no matter what roads or in what conditions. When you know that everything is made with a bigger idea or purpose, you cannot easily just quit.

For example, the purpose of my trip around South Asia (Pakistan, India, Nepal and Bangladesh) was to show this part of the world in a way that no one did before. Yes, I know that many people traveled in this area, but I am the first who has provided a detailed video series for the entire trip. I wanted to show you the real country, real people, real situations, and the real long motorcycle trip, not just the edited versions which will show you only the highlights and save you from the bad moments. As I have said so many times before, it's about being real.

I hope that all of the information I already published will be useful for many riders after me. This was my goal, and it helps me to complete the trip.

Tip N: 2 – Hope for the best and prepare for the worst

I can tell you this the other way around: **Prepare for the worst and hope for the best**, but I like the first the more. By saying this, I mean that you have to believe that it will be a trouble-free trip, but you also need to be ready to react if something goes wrong, and you have to be ready to react alone. Any help will be more than welcome, but you shouldn't rely on it. This actually reminds me of tip number 3, which is:

Tip N: 3 – Be careful with the bike choice

Here you might say: 'Pavlin, in almost every chapter you talk about the bike choice, why?'

Because it is so important! The whole trip will depend on the bike you going to have. It is a motorcycle trip, don't you forget. With this, I don't want to say that you have to buy the most expensive machine, no! You have to choose the right bike, the one which you can ride and control alone in any riding conditions. Good or bad roads, dirt, sand, gravel, mud or anything you can imagine.

Please do not tell me that you are planning to stay only on the asphalt because on the long trips you never know what you are going to face.

Tip N: 4 – Find the right tempo

When you travel alone, you have to find the right balance between the riding speed and the timing. If you are too slow, the time is not going to be enough, if you are too fast, you risk having an accident. Always keep in mind that you are alone and even a simple drop or wrong decision could ruin the whole trip. Long stops are not something I recommend, but if you think that you need it, just do it. It is very important to split your power for the entire trip, not only for a day or two.

Tip N: 5 – Never leave the bike unattended

This is one of the downsides to traveling alone. Never leave the bike unattended. Even if you just go to pay for your petrol, always take the key with you. Keep the most important things, like your passport, money, and your phone in your pockets at all times. The expensive items like cameras, GPS or any other electronic devices, you can keep in the tank bag, and if necessary take it with you. Do not trust in the simple lock that you might have on your hard cases or top box. They can be easily opened, even with a simple screwdriver.

Tip N: 6 – Be careful with money

Never show your money in public places. If you need to draw or change money, always do it in the big banks, not in small machines in a dark street. People around the world are great, but cash can be a very powerful stimulant for many, and you don't need to risk it. Keep a small amount in your pocket the rest, hide somewhere else.

Tip N: 7 – Walk around with confidence

Do not be afraid to talk with the locals, they are not going to bite you. 99% of the people around the world are great, but if you are unlucky enough to meet this other 1%, it will be only your fault because you probably looked like a victim. Even the most famous predators like the tiger for example, will always attack the weakest animal. With this, I am not talking from the position of a tall person. You can be a big guy and still look like a victim. Confidence is what you need.

Tip N: 8 – Never risk more than you can handle

You shouldn't do it even if you travel in a group, but it is far more important when you are alone. I mean for everything, not only for motorcycle riding. For example, do not go hiking in a place you don't know. Do now swim in a dangerous or remote beach. Do not argue with the locals if you cannot fight. Never put yourself in a situation that you cannot handle alone.

Tip N: 9 – Be consistent and patient

Good results always come with consistency and patience. Do not try to beat the time by taking unnecessary risks. You are not going to be the first to try to do this, but you will definitely will be the one to regret after that. With this, I mean the entire trip, not about the momentary speed.

Tip N: 10 – Enjoy the trip

Enjoy every single moment of the trip. Bad weather could become the most interesting part of the whole journey. A flat tire or a breakdown situation could result in you meeting new friends. Overnight stays in a shared hostel room might be the best experience you ever had. Actually, you never know where the adventure will come from! Enjoy your time, and you will be addicted forever, or at least this is what has happened with me.

*****

Tips for group riding

If for any reason you don't want to do it alone, that's absolutely fine; riding in a big group could be great fun as well. As usual, I will now give you 10 very useful tips about how to be the person everybody likes and tell you how to enjoy the trip at the same time.

As you know already, I have never been a fan of big groups, but there are always some exceptions. It really depends on you and your individual expectations.

For example, if you expect that everybody will listen to you because you are a great rider or the other way around, and you need help all the time because you know nothing, in both cases, you will be disappointed. Without compromises from both sides, it is not going to work.

Before I start with the tips, I will bore you with another personal story:

During my last trip to South Asia in Bangladesh, I had the chance to ride in a big group, 7 people actually. This was something absolutely new for me, something I never did before, I mean for a long period, not just for a couple of hours.

So, there were 7 people, we rode together, we ate together, and we shared the same room every single night and guess what? I really enjoyed myself!

The difference between the groups I have been in before and this particular group, was that they had a clear structure. They had a leader, a person who rides in front and who takes care of the logistics, they had a person who dealt with all the payments. Actually this was new for me, but I liked it so much.

From time to time, we just gave a certain amount of money to this person, and he was paying all the bills. Hotels, restaurants, coffees, and anything else we needed except petrol. He was the person who was going around and negotiating all the prices for us.

Another one was looking for the attractions we could see on the road. Also, a person who cares about all the camera gear. Even an entertainment person, I gave him the nickname Bollywood, because he was taking selfies all the time, and a guy who was responsible for some social connections. They were actually like one very well organized company.

They actually gave me an idea of the first tip:

N: 1 – Find your place in the group.

If you have ridden a motorcycle for a while, you should know what you can or what you cannot do. Find your place in the group and try to be helpful to everyone. Use your powerful sides to improve the timing, the mileage or just to support the rest of the riders. I just gave you an example of the many different positions you can find in any group.

Tip N: 2 - Learn how to make compromises.

This is something very important, and you have to find a way to overcome it. You are not the sun, and the universe is not going around you. You might suggest different routes or tactics, but please do not insist on being always right. Everybody makes mistakes, and you are no exception. Listen what the rest of the riders want to say and decide together what will be the actual plan.

Tip N: 3 – Be ready to travel alone.

I should have started with this, but it is never too late. Okay, this is something that you have to predict before the trip. Make your back-up plan, or at least prepare everything in a case that you need to travel alone. You need to have a plan, a whole strategy of how you are going to continue if you don't like the group. You don't need to make the plan at the last moment because it will finish even worse than the original group ride.

Tip N: 4 – Do not be arrogant.

You are just a man. A man with a head, two hands, two legs, and you are the same as everybody else. If you have more experience, great! Use it to help those who need help at any moment. Be like a father and not like a big brother, I guess you know what I mean.

Tip N: 5 – Do not imitate.

If you find yourself in a situation that is beyond your riding skills, do not try to imitate. I will repeat, **DO NOT TRY TO IMITATE!** This could end really badly, and it's not going to help to the rest of the riders at all. Ride at your own pace. If you are in the right group they will wait for you, if not, just use option 3 and continue alone.

Tip N: 6 – Be on time

Learn how to wake up fast. How to load and unload your bike as quickly as possible. Do not be the person who everybody needs to wait for. If you know that you cannot go without your 40 minute morning toilet break, then wake up 40 minutes earlier.

Tip N: 7 – Do not talk too much.

Even if you love your voice and you think that you are a great person, I will suggest to avoid the long speeches until you start your political career. It is good to be part of every conversation, but not to be the only one who speaks. Be part of the group, not the voice of the group.

Tip N: 8 - Accept your position.

This is something that is so important, and most of the confrontations will happen because of that. For example, you believe that you are the leader, but the group decides that you are better with something else. You might suggest some changes or offer some alternative solutions, but do it by following the tips I have said so far.

Tip N: 9 – Socialize with the group.

This is a bit of a tricky job, but you need to socialize with the group, not with your phone. Yes, it is understandable that you will need to make some phone calls to the family and check your e-mails, but do not convert the trip to something you can do later at home. I know that this is very hard, especially for young people who cannot even breathe without their smartphones and have a panic attack when they are not around, but…

Tip N: 10 – Focus on the important part.

By saying this, I mean to ignore anything else and focus on the important part. It is almost guaranteed that when many people are involved there will be some problems. Try to avoid it and do not even think about it. Believe it or not, they will disappear as soon as you lose the tension. If not, as I have already said – use option 3 and travel alone. That's it, nothing more. This should be more than enough to decide what you would like to do.

PART TWO: WHAT YOU REALLY NEED?

You made it! Congratulations! You have finished the first part of the book, and I really hope that it will push you to think in the right direction! But I am still not finished. In the second part I will share with you everything I have learned from so many hours spent on the motorcycle saddle. As usual, I will keep writing and advising in the same minimalist style, because I am what I am. This is the way that works well for me. I cannot see any reason that it won't work for you as well! Let's jump on to part two!

The definition of the best adventure motorcycle?

The word "adventure" has become very popular in the last few years, even my Youtube channel is named: "Motorcycle Adventures." The word "adventure" sounds very powerful and no doubt, we all love it. Motorcycle companies know that as well, and they use very cleverly to attract us to their new models. There are many variations at the moment, but what is really the definition of an adventure machine?

I will start with the definition of adventure:

'It is unknown, and exciting experience usually involving some risks.'

Did you hear something about a motorcycle? No, me neither. The adventure is a very special state of mind, and it could be reached with almost anything. Walking, running, cycling, riding motorcycles, racing, base-jumping, swimming, diving, horse riding, wild safari, climbing, and many more; for some people, it could be an adventure to go to the park...

I will give you one funny example: Last year, on my way to Bulgaria, because it was so cold and I had so many layers under my motorcycle clothes, to go to the toilet was already an adventure!

A motorcycle is just a tool, a vehicle to deliver the state of mind as I already told you. I know that this sounds very philosophical, but this is the reality. With this, I am not saying that you shouldn't have your preferences or that every bike is the same, no. What I am trying to say, is that almost every bike could be converted to an adventure machine.

There are so many examples on the internet for people who ride around the world with some of the so-called improper models; like a Yamaha R1 or 50cc scooter. There is simple proof that it could be done with anything, as long as you like it and want it.

However, we all have some preferences about how an adventure motorcycle is supposed to look like. I cannot talk in the name of all riders around the world, but I can tell you what I think.

What are my requirements? What do I expect from my adventure motorcycle? I will repeat this to avoid any misunderstanding – my adventure motorcycle! Yours could be absolutely different, and there is nothing wrong with it. It is like women, we all like different types!

N: 1 – Reliability.

This is the most important factor for me. Anything else, like great design, super powerful engine or cool features, it doesn't matter if the bike is not reliable. The design is the last thing I will want to see when the bike stops. The powerful engine means nothing when it doesn't work. The features are a useless piece of technology when you are stuck in the middle of nowhere.

N: 2 – The weight.

I have said this thousand of times, but I will say it again:

The weight always matters!'

As I said at the beginning, this is what I need from my adventure motorcycle. If you think that bigger and heavier is better, I understand and respect your choice. You will be the one who needs to deal with the weight of your model. Just make sure that you can lift your bike at least a couple of times alone, without any help. Keep in mind that when you try this at home, in a garage is one thing, but on the road with your entire luggage, when you are exhausted, in possible hot or cold weather, that things could be totally different. I will not even mention the moments when you will find yourself under the bike.

N: 3 - Possibilities to load luggage.

It is obvious that if you have the idea to travel with this motorcycle, you will need it. As you already know, I travel light, but even the amount of luggage I carry requires a strong frame and subframe. Especially, if you have an idea to leave the asphalt roads. The frame and the subframe will be exposed to a lot of shaking, and they could give up much faster than you could imagine. This is something I always have in my mind without sacrifice, is the total weight of the bike when it is loaded up.

N: 4 – Wheels

In my case, because as you know I love to include at least couple of km off-road in my trips, I prefer to have a 21-Inch front 17 or 18 on the back and spoke wheels. This will give me the chance to ride much more easily on the raw terrains, without damaging the wheels, but I will still be able to do it fine on the highways too. I know that for many of you it doesn't matter, but as I said already a couple of times, these are my preferences.

N: 5 – Suspension

This is something very important, and most of the riders never think about it. They believe that it is a matter only if you have to ride off-road, but this is not true. Every time when you twist the throttle, when you press the brake, or you go into a corner, the suspension is responsible for making it trouble-free and for keeping your wheels on the ground. Actually, if we have for example, two of exactly the same bikes, the same weight, frame, engine, wheels, but with different suspension, you will feel a significant difference in the riding control. It will be like a totally different bike.

That's it, nothing more. Anything else, like a bigger tank, tall windscreen, protection, better lights or any kind of adventure features could be easily added later if you have the basics I just told you.

My advice will be to choose and customize the bike exactly for your needs. Do not listen to what others will say, because in the end, you will be the person who is going to ride it, lift it, fix it, and take care of it.

'Pavlin, please go back to the question':

What is the best adventure motorcycle? Does it really exist?

Okay, let me see what I can tell you. For one person, the adventure will be to ride to the next town, but for another, it could be to go around the world. It is very subjective and really depends on the point of view of the individual, and the experience we have. If you are doing this all the time, it will become like something normal, and it is not an adventure anymore.

With all of that being said, what is the best adventure motorcycle? Is it a GS1250, KTM 790, Africa Twin or the new Yamaha Tenere 700?

Well guys, every time when I hear this question, I start to laugh. This is because there is no one simple answer! It doesn't matter what the so-called riding experts, magazines or famous Youtubers will say because each one of the answers will be based on one, or a few different perspectives and experiences.

I receive at least 10 e-mails per week from guys asking me the same question or looking for some kind of encouragement that the bikes they have got are good enough for their adventures. I usually will reply back that every bike will do the job with some simple modifications, and I seriously mean it.

Many people have already proven that you can travel with almost anything, even with small scooters. The size of the engine doesn't really matter as long you have the will to do it. It is obvious that around Europe, a bigger engine will be better, but it doesn't mean that you cannot do it with a small and simple bike.

I recently watched a video review of the Royal Enfield Himalayan. The guys tested the model for a couple of days in different terrains and came to the conclusion that it is not a proper adventure bike, because it was not good on the highways. Their presumption was that the adventure bike has to be great on any terrain.

You have to understand one very simple truth: **'This type of motorcycle does not exist!'**

No matter how much money you are going to pay or what brand you choose, there will be always pros and cons. 1000cc might be great for highways, but bad off-road. 250cc might be great for the dirt, but not so pleasant on the highways… ABS, TC, better food pegs, a bigger petrol tank, a tall windscreen, and all the adventure gadgets will make your journey more comfortable and safer, but they are not necessary.

The fresh examples I have now are from my last trip. In Pakistan, I rode a 250cc Benelli, naked bike. In India and Nepal, I rode a 400cc Royal Enfield Himalayan, the one that was labeled as not very good for adventures. In Bangladesh, I had a 150cc Lifan KPT, which most of you will consider to be a funny bike for teens…but, each one of the bikes did the job, and at the end, I came back home in one piece and with so many positive impressions.

Yes, they were never perfect, but all bikes are the same – never perfect. Good in one situation, bad or decent in another. Even my Yamaha, which I love, and which has brought me to so many places around the world sucks at many things. Every bike is just a compromise.

Let me give you a few more examples:

Some of the most popular adventure bikes are: GS1200, Honda Africa Twin, the old and the new model, Suzuki DR 650, Honda XR 650 and many similar. They are determined as the best adventure motorcycles, but I will tell you some simple facts that I have discovered recently on my last trip to South Asia.

In that part of the world you will face many problems:

N: 1 – You cannot find the proper tires. Yes, but you can bring your own.

N: 2 – You cannot find the proper oil. Yes, but you can bring your own.

N: 3 – You cannot find the spare parts. Yes, but you can bring everything you might need.

Helloooo, how much luggage are you planning to take, 100kg?!

N: 4 – You cannot find a mechanic to fix your bike. Yes, but you can learn how to fix it alone. Hmmm, okay.

Of course, the opposition: This is not true in the big cities like Karachi, Islamabad, Mumbai, Delhi, and Dhaka; here you can find everything! Oh really? This statement is far far away from the truth, but even so, are you planning to stay only in these cities or to ride around the country? Let me give you another example:

With the Benelli I had in Pakistan, at some stage in the North, I needed to change the oil, but I did not take oil with me, believing that there are motorcycles everywhere and finding oil shouldn't be a problem. Yes, but no. I cannot find even a simple bottle. They never heard about specifications MA or MA2 for a wet clutch. I was looking for something simple, 10W40 or 10W50 semi or full synthetic, but they don't have it. So I needed to ride the bike additional 1000km to Islamabad with the same oil.

Another point to consider is the garages and mechanics. They are basically working on the street, and they know what to do with the local motorcycles, but they have no idea how to fix your bike.

On the other hand, my friend Anif's bike, a Suzuki GS 150cc was not a problem and actually for this trip, he really did have the best adventure bike.

It was the same with the Himalayan in India, and the Chinese Lifan in Bangladesh. They were the best adventure bikes for the trip I did there.

Many guys asked me, did I miss my Tenere? Yes, I did, but when I saw all of this, I will never recommend that anyone go there with their own bike.

Another example I can give you is again from Pakistan. I met a nice couple Peter and Claudia from Austria. They were traveling with a Suzuki V Strom 1000. Two capital mistakes they made:

First, was that they have the wrong bike and the second that they were too heavy. They hit a big pothole in Afghanistan and bent the rim of the tubeless wheel and guess what? They easily lost a few days trying to fix the rim and finally, they continued their journey with a tube inside of the tubeless wheel. All of this could have been avoided if they just had a local bike. We talked about it a lot, and Claudia said – we are too heavy, 50% of the stuff we never used. Never again, next time they will travel with two light bikes.

Again, I have talked so much and said nothing. I think that I am ready to be a politician now. Let's get back to the topic.

The best adventure bike is the one that will help you to complete the trip with minimal effort and the fewest problems. The brand and model will both need to be carefully selected, depending on the destination and the type of the terrains you are going to ride.

Choose and prepare the bike for the hardest part of the trip, not for the easiest. For example, you can ride 150cc on the highways, yes, it would be slow, but you can do it, but with 1200cc on the dirt or sand, it will be very difficult and almost impossible for many.

Yes, you can always skip the difficult part of the trip and take some nice roads instead, but is this what you really want to do? What about if you don't have this chance? What are you going to do, stop, cry or pray to God to teleport your bike to the other side of the river for example?

Plan and go there with the idea to see the world, not to make pictures for Facebook or Instagram. By the way, I posted many already with the bikes I have at the moment, and no one criticizes the bikes I showed there. I said this before, and I know that many of you disagree, but it doesn't matter how much you love your bike in the end, it is just a tool, a vehicle to bring you there. The travel is what really matters!

Please remember it, and it will save you a lot of efforts and money of course.

*****

ABS or Not – Which is best?

Right here, right now, I can bet 100$ that you expect me to tell you how bad ABS is, because you can't use it off-road, because it's another possibility for a failed system in your bike or just because I don't have it, but....here you are, the biggest **BUT** again!

Did you ever hear the famous phrase?

'Everything that you are saying before BUT is shit, what you going to say after that is what really matters.'

As you know, I never talk just to listen to my voice. I told you already that the idea of this book is to help others to make the right decisions.

Now I know that I have totally confused you. I will bet even 200$ that you cannot even guess what I am going to tell you! Anyway, I think that you have waited long enough. Let's go back to the topic – ABS or Not?

My personal opinion is that the ABS is a great system and it should be standard to every motorcycle coming on the market today. It is the same with traction control, throttle control, uphill sensors, and many more systems. Especially if the bike has more than 100 H.P. All of this will help you to control it much easier and this could even save your life in many situations.

What about off-road?

Nothing, just turn it off when you don't need it. Even if it's not possible to switch it from the dashboard, you can always remove the fuse or even create a small manual switch. It's like a jacket in the summer – when it's hot, you just don't wear it.

Yes, but what about the extra kg, you always talk about the weight?

Modern ABS systems weigh no more than 1-1.5 kg. I think that you can remove many more far more useless things from your luggage than the ABS to compensate for this small additional weight.

Ok, but why do you ride a motorcycle without ABS?

There are two answers – long and short – I will go to the long because I hope that it will help you to get the idea of what I am trying to say:

I learnt how to ride motorcycles when I was just 15 years old. I did it the old fashioned way – by making a lot of mistakes until finally, I got it. I have tried many bikes and even rode dirt bikes for a couple of years. Every time that I fell down, I was learning why. Day after day, I finally realized how the brakes worked and what I should do to prevent these mistakes from happening again.

I learnt how powerful the front brakes are, but I also learnt how dangerous they could be. For me now, 30 years later, ABS is something really nice, but I can live without it. If it comes with the bike I like, then great, if not, it's nothing to worry about. The reason I chose the non-ABS version of my model was that the ABS version was heavier, with lower suspension travel and the battery is located under the tank. I hope this is clearer now.

What I like about ABS?

The first and the main thing has to be the safety. It could save your life, or at least a lot of money from accidents. Especially when the weather is not good – rain or even worse than this, in the snow or ice. The same goes for the traction control and the rest of the systems.

What I don't like?

I don't like the idea of something that takes control of my actions. As you know, most of the modern bikes are equipped with double brake systems. When you press the front, it activates the rear as well, or when you touch the rear, it does the front brakes at the same time. I know that this is very clever and it always knows what is the best in any situation, but I still refuse to believe it, and I still want to have my own control, to make my decisions, even if they are wrong.

In the end, it is just a computer and it takes the data from many sensors, and 95% of the cases will be right, but this 5% stuck in my mind.

As I said, the systems are great, but let's see what is the result of that. For the purpose of that experiment I will use one rider – John – random name – there is no real John behind the name.

Okay, John is a new rider, he just got a license and learned how to ride. Of course, he has a new bike, with all the new systems we have talked about. After a couple of years on the road, he will be experienced rider and will know very well when and how hard to press the brakes. On paper, this sounds good, but he only knows how to ride a motorcycle with ABS and a double brake system. What about if the system fails, or the fuses is burned. He will be on the road with the wrong skills entirely.

I will give you another example, a friend of mine has a big adventure bike. I will not say what brand, but he has a problem with the rear brake lever, I think perhaps it was a little bent or I don't know what exactly, but he said – I am all right because I never use it anyway… when I press the front, it brakes with the rear as well.

What?

So over the years, he developed this bad habit to use only the front brake.

A second example is from another friend of mine – in the last couple of years, he rode only new bikes. As a result of that, exactly like my other friend, he got used to it, and to the systems they have on those newer bikes. That's fine, but recently he decided to buy an older and lighter machine; this is because he has plans to go to Central Asia and he doesn't want to do it with the BIG ADVENTURE bike he has.

So he bought the bike and jumped on it to ride it home. He was happy because it was cheap, light, and he really enjoyed it. However, on one of the corners, a corner he was used to making many times, he pressed the front brake, as usual, but it locked, and he went into the ground without even understanding why! Luckily nothing really happened, but it is just an example of what could happen.

So finally, to make a conclusion:

I think that these are great systems, they should be standard, and everyone should be able to take the benefits from them, especially the newer riders. However, I highly recommend to anyone that you keep using the old-fashioned way of braking. The systems will work perfectly, you are not going to break it, don't even worry about it, but doing it you will increase your chances to stay unharmed in the case it stops working or you change the bike.

*****

Spoke Wheels or Alloy Wheels?

This is the question that many people have. How to choose the right model? To have nice and shiny alloy wheels or adventure looking spoke wheels? I will try to explain as simply as possible about the pros and cons of each one of the competitors.

The first motorcycles were nothing more than bicycles with small engines. In the beginning, they even used very simple wooden wheels. Then slowly, they moved to wire spoke wheels, and it was about the same until the late 70's, when I believe it was Honda who first designed alloy wheels. Since then, the revolution unfolded. Today, we can see thousands of different variations and models, actually, it is hard to choose, and you don't have to unless you have a very special custom bike.

Actually, if I ask you now, what is your favorite model alloy wheel, I can bet a 100$ that you cannot tell me, because you never look on the wheels. Who cares about that when you have a nice powerful bike? As I said, it is not important, but you have to know the differences between alloy and spoke wheels, and this is what I will try to explain now.

N: 1 - Alloy wheels.

You can see these on 99% of the sports bikes and on most of the touring bikes. There are a few reasons for this:

The first one is the design. Maybe you never pay attention to the different designs, but I am sure that in each one of the famous factories they have a special department that work on that, and every year, they spend thousands of dollars for new projects, tests, and colors. To have a brand new sports bike with simple wheels will be like to have a Gucci suit with old military shoes. They just don't match!

The second reason, is that the sports or touring bikes are very powerful and alloy wheels could provide the necessary strength and shape to handle that power. With simple words, you can use a wider tire.

The third reason, is that with these type of wheels, you can use tubeless tires, which are very important for both sports and touring bikes.

Another reason, is that because they could be produced fully automatically, there is no need for manual labor, which reduce the production price of the bikes.

And last but not least is – Safety. They cannot really explode, even if you have a puncture, the pressure will only drop slowly. Which as you know, is very important if you ride on the highway.

These are all pros, so let's summarise it:

- Lower price.
- Different designs.
- Possibility to have a wider tire.
- You can run tubeless tires.
- Easy to repair with very simple kits, no need to remove the tire from the bike.
- Safety on the high speed.

Of course, as with anything else, they have some cons.

Number one, weight. Yes, they are heavier. Of course, if you have some custom design race wheel for $500, made from titanium or something like that, then maybe not, but in most cases, they will be heavier.

Number two is that it is easy to bend it or damage it, and when it happens, it will be almost impossible to repair. I have seen some guys heat it up and then try to restore the original shape and it could work for a simple scooter or some kind of cheap bike, but for a sports machine – no chance. Even a simple curve will affect the balance of the wheel, and this could be very dangerous, especially at a high speed.

Number three, they are not good for off-road riding. Off-road terrain can easily bend the rim, and then you are done. Tubeless tires cannot hold the air if the board of the wheel is damaged. A big hammer might help in some cases, but not always. Usually, these things will happen when you don't have any help nearby. It's called Murphy's law!

Let's see the spoke wheels now.

They are used mostly for off-road motorcycles. The main reason for that is because they are light and durable. You can see it in some road models like BMW Nine-T, they even use some real off-road tires, also on some scramblers; but it's because of the vision of the bike, I cannot believe that someone will actually try this machine off-road.

So, the pros:

- Light,
- Durable,
- Perfect for off and on-road as well.
- The spokes could be replaced in the case of any damage.

Cons:

The first one is very obvious – you need tubes. Which is fine, most of you will never need to change it, but when you go on a trip, you need to have a spare with you. Some of you might say that it is not necessary if you have a tire repair kit. Yes, but not always.

The second and very big minus for these type of tires, is that the tube could blow up while you are riding, and when this happens, you lose control of the bike. It will depend on the situation, but this could end dramatically. Let me tell you one more personal story.

Last year, I went on a simple two-day trip, and because of that, I did not take my spare tubes. I was riding on the highway at around 120 km/h when my front tube blew up. It was a really scary situation, and for a couple of seconds, I said to myself – that's it, it will hurt now! Luckily, I managed to stop, and after a few deep breaths, I saw that the front tire was completely flat. Of course, I had my tire repair kit with me, but after two hours, and more than 7 patches, it was still not holding the air. Later on, I found out that a piece of metal drilled the tire and stuck into it. Because the hole was big, the pressure dropped very fast, and until I stopped, it drilled many smaller holes on the tube.

So I was there, 250km away from home, but without a spare tube. I was on the highway, it was getting dark, and all of this traffic was passing me, I wanted to go but, first I had to fix all of the punctures, whatever number they were. As usual, I never go on a trip without my famous luck, so a German guy with a big trailer for horses stopped and helped me to move the bike and find a new tube. Actually, it is a really nice story, and I had a great time after that, but the lesson was learned.

The third minus, is that even if you have spare tire or repair kit with patches to fix it, on the side of the road, it is not always that easy. At least you should have some practice, or you can spend hours jumping like a chicken around your bike without any result.

Another one downside of the spoke wheels is that it is very difficult to clean it properly, I know that after the blow-up situation it seems like nothing, but some riders could find it embarrassing.

Enough for the spoke wheels, the third model…

Hold on for a second, I think they were only two, alloy and spoke wheels, right?

Not really, there is actually another option, which is becoming more popular in the last few years; it is tubeless spoke wheels. If you haven't seen or heard of them until now, basically, these are the well-known spoke wheels, but the spokes are attached to the edge of the rim instead of in the middle. You can see it on almost on all new travel bikes like the GS 1200, Yamaha Super Tenere, Triumph Tiger and any more. I think that these are the best option for an adventure trip because all of these things like spare tubes, patches, tire levers, and changing the tire on the road will disappear.

So my friend, conclusion:

Alloy wheels: Great for road trips or racing, not good for off-road.

Spoke wheels: Good for road and off-road, but a lot of cons.

Tubeless spoke wheels: Great for everything, but usually only coming with the new bikes. Difficult to find in the aftermarket to match your particular model.

*****

How much gear do you actually need?

I know that with this chapter, I will probably hurt some feelings, especially to gear lovers, but I will take those risks. I want to share with you my personal experience, and I hope that you will listen.

So the idea came from one picture of a funny comic that I found on the internet. I upload it on both Facebook and Instagram, and we had a lot of fun. Many people recognized themselves in this funny cartoon.

What it shows, is a guy who just bought an engine guard, mounted it, and then found out that there is more protection for light, side panels, crash bars etc., and decided to order everything, converting the bike to a real tank.

Yes, it is funny, but actually, I have some close friends who do exactly the same all the time. I keep saying: **"Stop buying and start riding,"** but they just don't listen. They are what they are!

What I want to do now is to stop you before you become that person! If you already are, I respect your choice, but it's not going to hurt you if you read this. Anyway, let's get to the point about how much gear we actually need? Good question, isn't it?

I will never believe someone who talks about healthy food, but is always sick, to a fat fitness instructor, or a poor man talking about business success. I always thought that when we want to convince somebody, the best way to do this is to show some personal examples. That's why I decided to tell you what I have and use all the time, and I hope that this will help you to take the right decisions.

I will start with riding gear. At the moment, I have two helmets. One I use all the time on all of my trips, and one in case I have a passenger. Somebody might say, yes, but what are you doing with the old. Nothing, instead of keeping them in the garage I give it to someone, sell it on eBay or just put it into the rubbish. If you ride often, then a good quality helmet will last two or a maximum of three long trips. After that, you have to change it. I cannot keep them all, because after 20 years, you will need one garage only for helmets.

Riding jacket and pants

You can make many experiments, summer mesh jacket, winter jacket, another one with good ventilation pockets, but not waterproof and four season waterproof with ventilation pockets. Four different options for the same purpose, to ride your bike.

If you remove the first 3, you will be left with a 4-season waterproof, ventilated jacket which will work in any conditions, never perfect, but just fine. By the way, it will be the same with the rest of the jackets – never perfect!

Boots.

The same story, how many do you need? 3,5 or 10, are you a fashion model or a motorcycle rider.

Gloves.

4 pairs are more than enough, one super heavy, one for everyday use, waterproof and one simple and light for very hot days.

Camping gear.

Everything I have is going into one very small bag. Tent, sleeping bag, mattress, pillow, and foldable chair. I used to carry a stove, but not anymore.

Here, I want to tell you something interesting that I have learned in the last couple of years. I know that many of you connect adventure riding with camping, but it really depends on the trip you going to make. For example: Around Asia, the guest houses, hostels, and even hotels are very cheap. For about 10-15 dollars you will have a room, dinner, and breakfast. I see no reason to carry my tent unless I really want to camp somewhere to enjoy the wildlife.

On the other hand, around Europe the hotels are expensive, and the tent will be a good alternative. The problem is, that you cannot make wild camping, because in most countries, this is forbidden, so you need to pay for a camping spot. Usually, it is between 15 and 25 euro per night. You might say, well, it is still cheaper than hotels, not really. If you are a group of two people, it will cost you around 50 euro. If you do your homework, you will be able to find a hostel or even a hotel for about the same price of the camping or a bit more.

Okay, let's say that you love camping and the tent will be a must-have item. You prefer to pay the same, but to have this independence. Okay, I understand and respect that, but why do you need the stove? To cook my food, what a stupid question! Well, in 90% of the paid camping spots there will be a kitchen, and you can cook your food there. In the other 10%, I think you can survive with dry food. The places where camping is free or the camping spots have nothing, the hotels are cheap. If you don't believe me go and find out for yourself.

So, before you start buying all of this so-called adventure things, please think twice.

Luggage

It doesn't matter what system you use; either a hard case or soft luggage, you cannot have two at the same time. A friend of mine converted his garage to something very similar to a motorcycle accessories shop. I always said to him that if he sells everything he had, he will be able to go around the world, or at least half of the world. What is interesting to me is that he keeps buying stuff. On the other hand, at the moment, I have one my horseshoe bag and one duffel bag. That's it.

Clothes.

I have three riding t-shirts, short sleeves, and one long sleeves. I don't have even thermo underwear, because I never use it; but let's say that it could be very useful. That's it. Three pairs of socks and underwear.

One tank bag. When I decide that the old is worn out, I will just replace it with a new one.

One hydration pack. You don't need an additional bottle next to your bed, just the same.

On the trips with me, I have also zip pants, walking shoes, a hat, switcher, and flip flops. Of course I have shower gel, a toothbrush, and a small microfiber towel.

In addition, I have headlight, a small knife, and just a few more useful and light things, and that's it.

This is actually everything I carry with me. Without most of the so-called must have adventure stuff' I was able to go to more than 60 countries and will continue riding in the same simple way.

More gear and expensive gear cannot guarantee you will have a better experience, but it will definitely bring you more weight on the bike and less space in the garage.

*****

The best luggage system

I can almost read your mind saying: 'I know you already, you don't like hard cases and soft luggage is the best for you!' Yes, yes, you are right, I prefer soft luggage, but that's me, and I am not going to travel by your bike. So, what is the best motorcycle luggage system? Good question, isn't it? To find out, let's first see the pros and cons of each one of the competitors.

I will start with the hard cases or panniers, whatever you want to name it.

Pros:

- *You can lock your stuff in it.*
- *They are waterproof.*
- *You can use it for many years.*
- *You can take more luggage.*
- *Low center of gravity.*
- *You can use it as a chair and table in the camping spot.*

Before I go to the cons, I want to say it again with my thoughts on each one of the pros:

- **You can lock your stuff in it.** Easy to be unlocked with simple tools, even a screwdriver.
- **Waterproof.** – Depends from the model. I have seen many cases full of water after just a few minutes of rain.
- **You can use it for many years.** You might, but also you might need to weld it or fix it many times.
- **Low centre of gravity.** – Depends of the model and the position, in some cases it is terrible. Also, do not forget that even the empty cases + the racks weigh at least 10kg.
- **You can take more luggage.** Which is already a mistake.
- **You can use it as a chair and table in the camping spot.** Take the TV and the fridge…

What I just did is to show you one different point of view. Now let's see the cons:

- Too bulky and heavy.
- Usually they are very expensive.
- Possible overloading.
- The risk to hurt or even brake yours or your passenger's leg.
- Too wide when you have to filter through the traffic.

Let's say it again with the opinion of someone who likes this type of kit:

- **Too bulky and heavy.** It looks cool and my bike is not light anyway!
- **Usually they are very expensive.** The price is not a problem and I can use it for many years.
- **Possible overloading.** And what? I have a passenger and I need all of that stuff…
- **A risk to hurt or even brake yours or your passenger's leg.** This is not true, it never happened to me, it is the opposite; it protects my legs because the bike cannot fall completely.
- **Too wide when you have to filter through the traffic.** I never do it, it is illegal.

Again, I just showed you that everything depends on the bike and the point of view. Yes, yes, yes, but with the soft luggage it is different. Is that true? Let's start with the pros first:

- Soft luggage is lighter.
- It is usually much cheaper.
- No more pros.

My point of view:

- **Soft luggage is lighter.** – Definitely.
- **It is usually much cheaper.** – Agree.
- **No more pros** – correct, but that's enough for me.

Another rider's point of view:

- **Soft luggage is lighter.** Yes, because you cannot take anything in it.
- **It is usually much cheaper.** – Depends on the brand and model.
- **No more pros** – Yes, that's why I have hard cases.

Cons of the soft luggage:

- You cannot have the same amount of luggage.
- They do not last for many years.
- You cannot lock it.
- They don't look that good.
- They are not waterproof.

My opinion about the cons:

- **You cannot have the same amount of luggage.** – I don't need to.
- **They do not last for many years** – Depends on the model.
- **You cannot lock it** – And what, I never leave the bike in the middle of nowhere.
- **They don't look that good.** – Who said that?
- **They are not waterproof.** – Depends on the model.

I don't need to play the same scenarios over and over again just to convince you that everything is subjective and depends on your personal preferences. What I, or hundreds of people will say doesn't really matter, because we all have different requirements and preferences.

So, what is the solution? Which motorcycle system is better, hard cases or soft luggage?

Before we get to this, I have to ask you couple of questions:

- What bike do you have?
- How are you going to travel, solo or with pillion?
- How long the trip will be?
- How much luggage are you planning to take?
- What exactly? Just clothes or an expensive camera and computer gear?
- What type of roads do you plan to ride; only asphalt or off-road as well?
- Where? Europe, Africa, Asia, Australia or America.

Now you can stop reading and answer the questions, don't worry about me, I will wait here….

You did it, Great! Now, buy what you need and go ride.

…What? I did not what? I did not tell you which system is better? I see…

I just asked you some very simple questions and you should be able to answer them in just few minutes. Check again your answers and they will show you what exactly you need!

If you travel with pillion and have 70-80kg of luggage, including some expensive camera gear or computers, it is obvious that you have to go for hard cases; on the other hand, if you are like me, and travel with the most important items only, I see no reason to have all of this extra weight on the bike.

- The best system is the one that will help you to finish the trip without the need to fix it on the road or buy additional bags to keep your luggage in place.

- The best system is the one that will stay safe in the place it needs to be, without adding too much extra weight and expose the bike and yourself to no unnecessary risks.

- The best system is the one that will be there like a part of the bike and you will never feel it.

- The best system is the one you can afford and use with pleasure.

Still no answer…

Of course not, I cannot reply for you all. It is your bike and your trip, do it the way you like! Even if you make a mistake, it will give you priceless experience for the next time.

*****

Read this before you start buying

I usually talk of the top this and the best that, like the best adventure gear or the top 5 things… but in this chapter, I will tell you about the worst things I have bought thinking they would be great, but they weren't.

Nowadays, in the era of the internet, it's so easy to buy everything you want from your home. Thanks to smartphones, you can do it anywhere, and at any time. Amazon even offers a one-click button. It is so easy and practical that we do it all the time and of course this leads to some not so clever deals.

Everybody make mistakes, and I am no exception! During the years, I bought some nice and of course some useless things. I did it because I was thinking that it would be a good idea, but it turned out to be the exact opposite.

1. Motorcycle seat pads.

I have tried them all. Soft, hard, gel even air hawk. They all work, but not in the way I expected. The worst of all was the gel pad. When I tried it in the shop it was so nice that I spent 50 euro without even thinking, and I was sure that it would help a lot; but what I found later on was the exact opposite. After 50km, I threw it away and never used it again. It could be something wrong with me, I don't know, but without it I was able to ride 5 times more effectively.

2. Bicycle underwear.

Well… almost every second rider will swear that the bicycle pants help, but I won't. The touching points of the bicycle and motorcycle seats are completely different. I am not going even to discuss the discomfort this elastic stretching material created on my balls.

3. Single pole tent.

I bought one because it was lighter and had better waterproof stats, but I missed the obvious things. The shape of the construction has some limitations.

- Firstly, it cannot be opened it unless you have some soft ground to stick the poles in.
- It is difficult to open when you are alone.
- Because of the triangle shape, the inside space is limited.
- It is not recommended for windy areas.

So, I sold it and bought a dome tent. A bit heavier, but much better in all the conditions I just said.

4. Two points crash bars.

A couple of years ago, I bought crash bars for my Yamaha Tenere. Actually, they were a really nice design, planned to stay almost invisible, and protect the radiator from side drops. They got my attention and I bought them, but when I mounted it on the bike, I realized that in the case of an accident, they will cause more damage than protection. On top of everything, the mounting plates were so fragile and on such a difficult to access spot that I left it there for more than 6 months praying that I am not going to drop the bike and damage things which I wouldn't have had to do if they were not there.

5. **Cheap waterproof boots.**

I bought a pair of waterproof boots for a good price. I am not going to say anything about the brand, but I will say that it is a well-known company with a good reputation here in Germany. On one of my trips, I had to ride in a temperature more than 40 degrees C. All day, I felt that my feet were boiling hot. Later in the evening when I removed the boots, I found out why. The company had made the boots waterproof by adding a piece of nylon between the leather and the lining. Yes, they were waterproof, but not breathable.

The decision was simple, I cut the linings and finished the trip, but I will never do it again.

It is good to watch some reviews and recommendations, but you have to keep in mind that what is good for one could be the worst for another. As you know my friend, the truth is always somewhere between. The best way to learn what you really need is to travel as much as possible. Even a simple weekend trip will give you an idea of what works and what doesn't.

*****

Motorcycle Safety Gear

As you know very well, riding a motorcycle is a dangerous hobby. Nothing is more important than our lives. To ride a bike without the proper gear is like taking a gamble with your luck. Sooner or later you will find out that you are just a human and that you need protection. In this chapter, I am going to talk about the most popular safety gear, and I will try to point out the pros and cons of each of the options.

I am guessing that even you, maybe once in your lifetime were reckless and rode a bike without any gear. I was the same when I was 20 years old. I was riding in the city at 200km per hour without even a helmet. My wife told me that I am a donor of organs. Anyway, these days are gone, and I will never do it again. The question now is what gear to choose, there are so many brands, varieties, and models, how do you pick the right gear for you?

As usual, I will tell you that it really depends on the type of bike you have and of course, on your riding style. For example, the leather suit is not going to be so comfortable on the motocross track; on the other hand, to have a plastic chest protector for high speed riding is no good either. To find out exactly what it is that you, need we have to see what are the options on the market today:

I am not going to talk about helmets because we all know how important they are.

Let's start simple: **Chest protector.**

It is usually used on either a motocross or dual sports ride. The main reason to choose this type of protection instead of the full body armor is to prevent serious bodily injuries in case you hit the handlebar, another part of the bike, or to stop stones flying directly to your body. Because they are made from a hard material, such as plastic or something similar, they protect the upper part of your body, your chest, and your shoulders from any direct impact. The second reason, is that they are very well ventilated, which is very important when you are racing for example.

The biggest con of this type of protection is, that as I said, they protect only the chest, partly the shoulders, and of course, the spine as well; but not in the way we expect it. If you hit the ground, for example, this protector will move on the side because it is supported only by a set of flexible straps; this cannot guarantee that it will protect you at all. Also for your elbows, you will need additional gear.

The second con is that they are big and bulky, which means that they are not so easy to wear under your jacket. Also, after a few hours ride, they become really uncomfortable.

As I said, they are great on the motocross track, but cannot really provide the safety we need on the street, and they are definitely not for long trips.

The second type: **Full body armor.**

This gear provides maybe the best protection for the upper part of the body. As you can learn from the name, full body armor, it also provides very good protection on the spine and elbows as well. It has a good chest protection and a wide kidney belt: when you tighten it, the gear cannot move and always stays in the places you expect them to be. Sounds like a great option, but of course, as with everything, it has some cons.

The first one, is that they are too tight and too hot for the summer ride. Even though they are made from mesh, they are just too hot.

The second minus is again the size. They are too big and bulky, and difficult to wear with a jacket on. I thought that when I removed the sleeves, I will be able to use it under my riding jacket, but it is not that simple.

Usually, the jacket and the pants have zips, you can actually zip them together, and this stops the cold wind from going under your clothes. My jacket even has two zips, one long zip for the pants and jacket; and one short, just on the rear side, but when I wear this armor, it is too low and goes on the top of my pants, so I cannot really zip it with my jacket. Perhaps this sounds like it's not a big deal, but believe me, when the temperatures drop it is not good at all.

Okay, so far so good, now we have to think about our knees.

The first option will be a simple knee protector. They are fine and provide very good protection for any direct impact because they are made from plastic. They have a joint in the middle so you can easily jump on the bike and even walk around with a moderate level of ease.

To fix it on your knees, they have flexible straps to tighten it properly. The idea behind this, is that the knee protector needs to go inside of the boot and become an extension of the boot and prove the maximum possible protection. Keep in mind, that in order to use these protectors without proper boots is equal to nothing.

The biggest con of these protectors is that they will not prevent your leg from being twisted or bent in the opposite direction. The second con is that because of their size you cannot wear pants over them. You will either need motocross pants, or you need to have it outside. I have seen some people do this before.

There is another one option, a knee brace. They are very similar, but they have been designed and made to be much better; they are not so bulky and provide excellent protection. The knee cannot be twisted or bent, the problem is that they are not cheap, the prices start from $400.

The third option will be: **Jacket or pants with integrated protection.**

What this actually means is that in your jacket and pants, they will have some kind of protectors on the risky zones. The shoulders, elbows, knees, and of course, one big one on the back protecting your spine. This is maybe the most convenient option to use of all. The reason for this is that it is already integrated into your gear. You don't need to carry additional stuff, which is really annoying, especially on a long trip.

I have tried all of the options that I just described and finally stuck with this because as I said, on the long trips any additional gear become a problem in some stage. A good example of that is when you just want to walk around the city. Where are you going to leave all of that stuff? Body armor, knee brace, Even if you have big hard cases they will not be enough to pack everything inside.

There is still one very important thing that you have to keep in mind. Regarding the latest safety requirements, these types of protectors provide the most necessary protection, but in reality, it is a bit different. For example, if the jacket or the pants are not exactly your number – perhaps they are a little bit bigger, the protectors can move inside, and the result will be not what you expect.

The last option I can point out to you is the Airbag system. I tested one of these at the Zurich International Motorcycle Exhibition, and I really believe that from a safety point of view, this is the best option at the moment.

There are two options, airbag vest, and jacket. The only con I found with both of these two is the price. It starts at 750 euro.

So, as I said earlier, each one of the options has some pros and cons. What exactly to take on your trips will be your decision, but keep in mind that the best protection for any accident is hidden deep inside of your head. You are the person who twists the throttle and presses the brakes.

*****

Buy proper motorcycle boots!

Let's talk about motorcycle boots now, are they really necessary? If you ever asked yourself this question, keep reading, and I will give you three, very good reasons to buy them.

People never stop to surprise me with these strange questions. Are these boots really necessary or can I ride my motorcycle with my hiking shoes? You can ride your bike with anything you want, even with thongs. Regarding the law, the only must-have protection is the helmet, and this is not even the case in all countries.

Regarding to the boots, some riders will say that they are necessary only if you ride off-road, really! What about if you slide on the street and your 300kg bike is on top of you? Or even worse, a car hits you from the side!

I have even seen videos on Youtube, from riders talking how bad the boots are, that they are not necessary and so on. For me, all of this is absolute nonsense! Any protection is better than no protection, it's so simple. The boots are part of your motorcycle gear, and you should wear them every time. The right question should be, what boots should I buy? Enough preaching, let's go to the top three reasons to buy motorcycle boots.

N: 1. Safety.

Nothing is more important than safety. Many people think the exact the opposite, and finally, they learned the hard way, by spending month after month in front of the television, thinking about their capital mistake. Don't play the same game, because sooner or later you will lose.

Let's just have a look at some of the popular options.

Hiking shoes. They have a solid sole, a nice cover, they are usually waterproof, comfy to walk around in, and they come in a variety of designs. They will protect your feet, maybe the ankle a bit, but nothing more.

The second is the standard touring boots. A nice leather cover, in most of the cases waterproof, some kind of protection on the toes and the heel as well. You can easily walk around, and that's why they are so popular on the market. Much better than hiking shoes, but still far away from having real protection. There are some exceptions like the Sidi Adventure boots, but even they are a nice compromise.

The third option is the heavy duty off-road boots. The difference between these and the touring boots is the hard materials they use. There is more plastic on the toe and the heel, a thick protection shield on the front part, a metal plate on the sole, which will give you great stability when you ride standing on the pegs. This combination will provide the best possible protection for your feet.

Of course the cons are many, too heavy, too bulky, hard to wear with pants on the top, most models are not waterproof and they can be difficult to walk with, and actually, you will be like Robocop. That's right, no comfort, but comfort and protection cannot really work together.

N: 2 - Suitable for any weather.

The second reason to wear motorcycle boots is that they are suitable for any weather. Yes, correct any weather. You can use them in the winter, but in the summer as well. Here you might say, hold on a minute, it was you who complained about boots, boiling feet, and so on. In the summer is too hot with boots! Really! Have you ever tried to ride a BMW GS 1200, the boxer, without boots in the summer? If you ever did, you will know what I am talking about.

Of course, you have to be careful about what you buy. Breathable materials are what you need. Gortex, Sympatex or whatever name you like.

N: 3 - Longevity.

Because you are going to use them in any kind of weather: cold, hot, and in the rain as well, you will wear it them for many hours, and in some cases, it could b days without taking it off. When you add all the dust, mud, petrol, oil, and other substances, don't think that you will find a shoe that has the same longevity. It doesn't matter how much you are going to pay for it, it will be one of the best investments you have ever made.

Remember, even the cheapest motorcycle boots will provide you significantly more than the most beautiful air.

*****

How to film your adventures?

We all know how to shoot a nice action moment, just press the button and go – easy peasy, but it is a different story when you have to record a long trip, week, month or more. The information I am going to give you now will help you to prepare, organize, and record your trip as easily as possible.

I decided to write about it because I have received many questions on this exact topic. So many people suggest what gear I have to use in the name of better quality, but the problem is, that most of them have never even done this before! I mean to film the whole trip, from the beginning until the end, day by day. If they try, they will soon realize that most of the advice they gave me won't work, or at least not in the way they expect. With this, I am not saying that because I have a couple of videos on YouTube that I am very good, no, I just wanted to share with you what I have learned from making those videos.

Before you even start, you should have a clear idea of what exactly you would like to show on the video. I will now provide you with some easy to understand tips, and I hope that they will help you to make the videos you really want.

N: 1 - What are you going to do with this video?

First and very importantly, is to know what you are going to do with this video. Will it be just for you, for YouTube or for sale? If you know that from the beginning, you will prepare the gear you need to make it. For example, if you plan on making a full professional movie which you will then sell later on Vimeo, you will need a camera crew and much better gear, including some serious stabilizers, drones, and many more film gadgets. On the other hand, if the video is just for you and your friends, you can make it with anything.

For YouTube, you need to have at least the basic requirements at the moment, like a decent HD camera, shooting in 1080p, and to keep some chronological order if you want someone to watch your videos later.

N: 2 – The gear is not everything.

Yes, correct, the gear is not everything. I will use one phrase from the famous photographer Ken Rockwell:

'Buying an expensive camera does not make you a great photographer, it just makes you the owner of an expensive camera!'

There are so many things that you have to learn before you can even start filming, like rules of thirds, lighting, exposure, and many more. Actually, once you start, you will realize that you know nothing. There are some really great stories, and videos that have been shot with very simple gear, but they are so good. Do you think that this is just an accident? No! The guys who did it, they knew exactly what they wanted to see on their footage, and the result is proof that the gear is not everything.

N. 3 – Learn how to use the gear you have.

It is so important to know the possibilities and limitations of your camera. For example, GoPro's are great cameras in terms of video quality, accessories, and features, but their functionality as a helmet camera is terrible. Now, of course, I expect you to resist and tell me: No! GoPro is the best! You can use a remote control, mobile app, you can charge it from power bank, or many more…

I know, but all of these things are only good for a 30 minute action clip. It's a different story when you have to record one week, one month or a one-year trip, especially when you are a one-man-show.

N: 4 – Learn what people want to watch.

Again, if the video is just for you, this doesn't matter; but if you have an idea to share your footage, then it will need to be different. A 10-minute set of footage from your helmet camera about how you ride is going to be really boring for your wife and kids for example, but if you mix it with the dinner you had, and the hotel room décor, I guarantee you that they will watch it.

The human brain is a very complex machine and it is always looking for something new, something different. Change the scenes more often, do not hold the same angle of view for more than 10 seconds. Learn from a famous movie or from commercials. Change the camera's perspective, and use two or three different cameras mounted on different spots. Have this in mind from the moment you shoot it because it will be difficult to edit later if you don't have any idea where this part will go.

N: 5 – Storytelling.

I should have started with this, but I kept it until last because I hope that you will remember it better. It doesn't matter how good the quality of the video is if you have no idea what it is about. The final result will be not what you expect. Every video should have some basic structure: A beginning, an important part, and an ending. The viewer needs to be taken on a journey with you, not just dropped in the middle of nowhere. It needs to be done gently and slowly, no rushing. Sometimes, expecting something to happen is better than a real event at the end. I am not saying that you have to lie and keep them watching for nothing, but it should have some balance.

It's a bit different when you make a series, like my last travel videos; then you have this in mind when you make the footage. Otherwise, it will be difficult to split it later.

Bonus tip – Music for your video.

Find the proper music. The same footage with proper music will be much better than without any music. I know that many will prefer to listen to the engine noise instead of music, but how many great Hollywood productions have you watched without a soundtrack? You can add it in some places, but not all the time. You can control the volume level, cut the scenes to match to the beat, and much more...

My favorite movie, the one I made, was from Central Asia. It was done with a single helmet camera that cost only $200. The quality is not so good, the audio missing in many places, it was recorded many times, again and again because of the copyright strikes. So finally, I needed to add different songs than what was in the original plan, but even with all of the changes, it is still a great video. It has more than 200,000 views and more than 2,000 likes. Keep in mind, that the videos were deleted and uploaded many times, because of the copyrights I told you, so actually it has more than half a million views. And this is a one hour film, not a 5 minute action clip. I still believe that all of this is because of the music. It just matched perfectly with the countries we have been to. Many people said that it was horrible to listen to these songs, but I thought that this was the best way to show you this part of the world. You can watch it on my channel, and I would like to hear your comments after that.

Alright, I told you how to make the video, and this leads us to the next question:

How and where to store your adventure video files?

Okay, the question I receive very often is: How am I able to store all of these video files? Hours and hours of riding, day after day, month after month... How and where can I store all of the files? Well, the answer is very simple, and this is what I am about to tell you now.

I keep all the files on SD cards. They are small, easy to keep in my pocket, and they almost never fail. In the past, I may have had a couple of video files corrupted, but it is more than likely everything will be alright doing things this way.

And now the question: Okay, fair enough, but how many SD cards will I need to record such a trip, 50, 100, 200 or more? No, actually I have the whole of the South Asia trip on only 17 SD cards. 14 x 32GB, 2 x 64 GB and 1 x 128 GB, which makes around 700GB. I shoot in 1080P, and regarding my cameras, it's around 9 minutes per GB, which means that with 700GB, I would be able to record 6,300min or 105 hours.

Usually, I ride around 10 hours per day, so if I record everything, I will need at least 6 batteries and 6 GB per hour, which means 60 GB per day. For a two month trip, I will need at least 7,000 GB! Without even including the other static videos I have recorded while I am not riding, like around the towns or meetings with friends...

So after I already told you that, it becomes perfectly clear that there is no way to record everything. Even if you do it, in the end, you are going to have a huge amount of useless files and how are you going to edit it?

Again, instead of giving you the answers, I only ask questions! I apologise for that! The trick is to record the most important moments from the trip. For example, there is no point to record two hours riding on the highway, or the whole day, because it will be too boring.

'Okay, but how do you know which are the important moments? What about if I miss something? '

Yes, you can miss something, like I miss the ditch in Scotland or my battery died on the Rohtang Pass in Ladakh. This is the situation. There is no perfect world unless you have a camera crew to take care of all of these things.

What I usually do is to turn on the camera when I see something interesting, or when I ride in difficult terrains or similar situations. I turn on the camera for a couple of seconds or minutes, depending on the situation. Basically, what you see in my videos is what I decided to record. I always try to keep some logical way to tell you the whole story. Where I am at the moment, what are the next steps, just to keep the viewers updated. If I jump from a ride in cities and then into the mountains, you might ask: How the hell did you get there? How long was the ride? Is the road good? and many more.

The whole idea of my videos is to show you the world the way it is. More like the documentary type of movie. Not much editing, no special effects, no cinematic views. It is very easy for me to cut only the highlights, add some cool music, and make the whole trip to look like a super hardcore adventure, but this will be far from the reality.

On a long motorcycle trip, you will face a lot of boring riding hours, bad weather, and not so many pleasant situations. I want you to know the reality. I also believe that this information could be very useful for everyone who has plans to ride in the same direction. Because I am a one-man-show, I always try to keep it as simple as possible. This helps me to edit the videos much easily after that.

Another reason to keep it simple is to record the whole trip with just one or two cameras. This is what I do instead of using multiple camera angles and different points of view. I use it sometimes, but not all the time. All of this could be done for short video clips of perhaps 5 to 10 minutes, but I cannot make it for the whole trip. It would be too much work and almost impossible to find exactly the position of every video file after that.

Here you can say that if I check the date and the time on the file, I will know where exactly it needs to be. Yes, but I came back with thousands of files. Who is going to check them all? Don't you forget, I am a one-man-show!

I hope that you get the point! Okay, let me tell you where I keep the SD cards. I purchased two small plastic memory card holders. They are very light, and look like credit cards. Each one holds 10 SD cards.

The reason I keep everything here, instead of just dropping them altogether in a box is that these holders give me the chance to mark the SD cards. To be able to follow the logical order and find the days I need much easier after that.

Another very important moment is that I need these cards to be always in a safe place. Can you imagine, after talking for two months about the longest video series, I then tell you that I lost my cards or my bag was stolen or something similar? I promised that I will deliver a detailed video series and I cannot afford to lose the cards. That's why I always kept it in my wallet in my pocket. Even though my jacket is waterproof and I kept the cards in another sealed plastic bag, to prevent any damage.

The reason I use many 32GB instead of a few 128GB are few. Firstly, is that my Contour camera (my helmet camera) supports a maximum of 32GB. Secondly, is that the tablet I use to upload the video updates in YouTube is also for a maximum of 32 GB, and the last reason is that even if the card fails I will lose only 32GB instead of 128GB. Actually the biggest cards, 64 and 128GB, I used just to add some additional files likes the videos from my Bangladeshi friend's cameras, drone, and many more. I also used one 64GB SD card for all of my pictures, and I have around 1,000 RAW files from this trip.

I hope that this information will be useful for you and will help you to make the adventure videos you always wanted to do!

*****

Do I need a tank bag?

Well... this is a question you have to answer, not me! It really depends on your personal preferences. For me, the tank bag is the most practical luggage system. Firstly, because it stays on the tank, which means that the weight is well distributed. The second, is that because of the position of the bag, I can see it all the time, and there is no way to lose it. The third is because I can always easily take it with me when I am not on the bike.

Another reason for me to always have a tank bag is because I keep all of my camera gear inside. The pros I just mentioned work perfectly for me. Many people prefer to have a top box for that purpose, something like a Pelican camera gear case, which is well made, with a foam inside and locks, but as you already know, I don't like top boxes. Also, I don't think that it is a good idea to place so much trust on the locks they have, especially if you carry expensive camera gear. They can be very easily unlocked with simple tools like a screwdriver.

So, what do I have inside?

All of my camera gear, as I told you already. Three different cameras, tripods, cables, batteries, and microphones. I also have my point and shoot camera, and this is basically everything I need to make my videos.

Aside from that, I have a second pair of gloves. For example, if I ride in the cold days, I have spare light gloves inside. If it is hot, it is the other way round. I also carry my favorite cap, some simple tools, like flashlight, a compass, and a few more everyday use items. In the big transparent pocket, I keep the maps, and this is pretty much everything I have inside.

So, do you need a tank bag? I don't know, you tell me.

*****

What do I have in my motorcycle saddle bag?

I am always preaching to go as light as possible, less is better, the weight always matters, but I never really told you what exactly I have in my saddle bag.

In fact, I did it in my first book, but it was made a long time ago, and that's why I decided it make it again. Also, since then, most of my preferences have been changed, and now I carry even less. Believe it or not, you actually don't need that much to travel.

Alright, most of you prefer to have some extra clothes or shoes, and in the end, they finish with 50kg of luggage with things which they might need. Please do not miss the important fact that you are going to travel on our planet, not on Mars. In every town or village, it doesn't matter where exactly it's located or how big it is, you will find clothes or shoes. The things that are usually hard to find, and it is better to have these, are riding gear, boots, and they actually do not stay in your bags.

Everything that I have inside you can easily spread out on a small table. You might say that this is not really true, but everybody who has met me on the road will confirm that. So actually I have:

- Three pairs of socks.
- Three sets of underwear.
- Three riding t-shirts, short sleeves.
- One long sleeve.
- One switcher.
- Two hiking pants, very light with a zip, so I can remove it in the case it becomes too hot.
- Walking shoes and thongs.
- Two towels, small and big.

- Small foldable backpack and also this small belt bag to carry my camera gear while I walk around.
- Toothbrush, paste, soap, dry stick, and laundry gel.
- I also carry some spare parts in a small plastic box.
- Two tubes, 21 and 17 Inch.

In this bag, I can also put my tent in the case if I need it. Everything, the tent, the mattress, the pillow, the sleeping bag, and even a small foldable chair is here, and the weight is 4.5 kg. On the last trip, I didn't even need it. I used to carry a stove and some cooking stuff, but not anymore. So, everything altogether, the clothes, the spare parts, and the tent, it's around 15kg.

I use to split all of these in different bags, so this actually gives me the chance to find it easy and take only what I need. For example, if I sleep in a hotel and the bike is stored in parking or garage, I do not take the whole bag, only what I need. Sometimes, when I arrive later in the evening and I don't have any plans to walk around I just take my toothbrush and the soap and go to sleep.

All the tools that I might need in case of a breakdown, my tire repair kit levers, and much more will always stay on the bike, not in the saddle bag. In case I need it, they will be always there, and it doesn't matter what luggage I have at the time .

All of my camera gear, chargers, and anything else I need on the road stays in my tank bag. So the whole luggage, the saddle bag, and my tank bag are less than 20kg.

You might say: 'Pavlin, I need much more than that, because of this or that…!'

Seriously? You need it, or you might need it? These are two different things!!

*****

PART THREE: GET READY FOR REAL ADVENTURES

So far so good! You came to the final part of the book which means that you are ready for the real adventures! I will use another famous phrase:

'When the road ends, the adventure begins!'

If you are looking for adventures, sooner or later you have to leave the asphalt roads. I am sure that you will love it, but the beginning is always difficult. With that being said, let's jump into the next chapter:

Off-road modifications

Here, I will now talk about the basic modifications you need to do if you want to ride your bike off-road. I will tell you some very practical tips and hacks on how to convert your motorcycle to a real adventure machine. The most important thing is that I will tell you how to do it without the need to rob a bank!

I have read a number of opinions and even seen a couple of videos on Youtube and the guys their advice to buy some really expensive stuff, in the name of the adventure.

Usually, behind the person or the camera is sat a huge GS Adventure, Yamaha Super Tenere or KTM. Of course, loaded with hard cases and hundreds of expensive gadgets, which will allow you to make your desired adventures! They will try to convince you that if you have specific gear, you can do whatever you like.

Is it really like that?

I am sorry my friend, but I will disappoint you! To ride any bike over 120kg off-road is not an easy job and almost impossible for many people. It doesn't matter how expensive the bike and the gear are, the weight is just too much. Even my bike, which weighs 200kg loaded with 22l of petrol is way too much to do any serious off-road riding. I can ride it on some dirt roads, sand, mud, and even snow if necessary, but the possibilities are limited. If you know that right from the beginning you will save a lot of money buying useless stuff trying to reach an impossible destination.

What I will tell you now is how to make some basic adjustments. They will not make you better off-road rider, but they will improve your riding comfort off-road.

First and most important is to make some small changes. Which means that you have to make the bike as light as possible. Take out all the stuff you don't really need. **Remember that weight always matters!**

If you always ride alone, remove the rear foot pegs as well. Believe it or not, on my bike they are very heavy and actually weigh about 2 kg. Forget about the hard cases or top box, they will not survive the bumps. Keep it simple, less is always better.

After all of this is done, you can add some necessary weight like an engine guard. This is something very important. No compromises. Buy the best you can afford or make your own.

The foot pegs are something really important. They need to be wide enough to support your weight when you stand on the bike. The one's I have are nothing special. Actually, I bought them from eBay for $10. They were not for my model, and I had to make some simple modifications, but they have served me well for many years.

You will also need a better handlebar and bar risers. This will give you the chance to ride on the standing position, which is the most important thing if you want to learn how to control the bike.

The next step will be to adjust the levers, clutch, front, rear brakes, and gear shift. They need to be in the proper position to be used with motorcycle boots from the standing position.

It is the same with handlebar levers. The position while you ride on the seat and stand is different. One very simple trick is to leave it a bit loose so you can change it if you need to.

Of course, you will need hand guards to protect it if the bike goes down. Yes, if you plan to ride off-road, sooner or later you will go down, no exceptions!

The next necessary step is to upgrade the suspension. On my bike, I have made a lot of changes, but on yours, you don't have to. Do whatever you can afford, but at least the springs of the forks, with some stiffer or progressive phases. If you have a preloaded bolt on the tip, tighten it, If not, you can try to add some spacers on the top of the springs. Keep in mind that this will make the springs stiffer, but it will also make the spring travel shorter. It is the same on the rear shock. Change it if you can, if not tighten it.

No we came to the next important part - tires. You have to understand that the tires are what keep you straight. The difference between the same bike with and without proper dual sports tires is like the difference between day and night.

Buy the best model you can afford. They need to be at least 50/50 on off-road. 40/60 or 30/70 is even better. I will not recommend riding with knobblies because you will have problems when you go back on the asphalt.

Okay, job done, you made the necessary adjustments, and now you have to learn how to ride off-road. The best way, will be to join some off-road course and learn the proper way. If you cannot afford that, or you are just too shy to do it, I will recommend starting with some very simple attempts. In your back yard or smooth dirt roads. Nothing special, just to be able to feel the bike and to learn how it reacts on such terrain.

I will try to give you some really basic riding techniques, even though I told you at the beginning that I would not do it.

Firstly and very important is to learn that the throttle is everything. Yes, correct, this is what keeps the bike straight. When I was learning how to ride off-road, many years ago, a friend of mine said: If in doubt, twist the throttle, if you slide, twist the throttle, if you get stuck, hit something, lose balance or whatever happens, twist the throttle and you will be fine. More throttle is equal to a higher speed, which keeps your bike in the straight position.

The second important thing is to ride in the standing position. Once you learn that, the rest is easy. With the standing position, you will have better control of the bike, a lower center of gravity, better visibility, and a good chance to release the pressure from your boots. The important tip to remember, is that you need to keep your knees loose. Do not lock them! They need to be like shock absorbers, helping you and the bike to absorb the bumps and travel easier. The body needs to be a little bent forward, the knees a bit loose, and your chin will need to face to your handlebars.

Another important technique to learn is to keep control of the bike with your knees, not with your hands. This will help you to control it better, and ride for many hours without being tired.

When you stand, you actually move the bike with your feet. When you put more weight into the right peg, you will go to the right, more to the left and you will go to the left. I have seen some guys advise to ride standing on the corners, but this is something you cannot learn for a day or two. At the beginning, I will strongly recommend that before the corners, you always slow down and sit. To make a turn with a heavy adventure bike while you are standing will be very risky for you as a beginner.

Important! Never ever try to stop the bike falling down with your leg. This could be really dangerous. You cannot stop a 200 or 250kg bike if it slides! You will be more likely to break your leg. Do not look at the guys from the motocross track, they use their leg for balance, not to support the bike.

Always brake before the corners. Once you are inside, do not chop the throttle, keep it steady and twist it slowly once you finish the maneuver. Let the tires to do their job.

If you have ABS or traction control, turn it off. Use the front brake only if the bike is straight, never ever press it on the corners. I know that coming from the streets, this is the first reaction you going to have, but you have to learn it, or you will suffer. The rear brake could slide as well, but it will give you some reaction time as the front will put you down immediately.

If you need to ride on the sand, reduce the pressure of the tires first. Keep your seating position as far back as possible, this will give you more traction to the rear wheel and release the weight from the front.

Keep your feet on the pegs, not on the ground. This is actually the most critical moment! If you do it, the front will start to shake and you will be ready to go down. It will shake because with every step you make, you actually move the weight from left to right without even noticing it. Keep your feet on the pegs.

And something else that is very important to remember! When you ride on the sand, you need more throttle. Did you listen when I told you that the throttle is your friend? Start with the first gear, very gently and change into second as fast as possible. Try to keep a steady speed. Fast enough to keep you straight, but not so much that you lose control of the bike. The speed will keep you straight and will not allow you to get stuck. If it's happened, do not twist the throttle! Cut the engine, lay the bike on the side, and lift it again in a different position.

That's it, now go ride!

Remember, the more you practice, the better you will become.

*****

Motorcycle trips in the winter

After I made the winter trip around the Balkans, I received a lot of questions. How I was dressed, what gear, what tires, how I ride and many more. I decided to talk about it and explain to you in more detail about what you have to do, if you need to ride in the winter. I will repeat, **if you have to,** because this is not something I will recommend.

Let's make it clear from the beginning. I will talk about a long trip, day, week or more, not for daily commuting. There is a big difference between these. It is one thing to get dressed for a 30 minute ride, and it's totally different when you have to spend eight or more hours riding is these conditions and to do it day after day, just keep that in mind.

The first piece of advice I can give you, and it is actually the best – **Don't do it!** Sounds really confusing, from someone who already made it, but I want to protect you from everything I have already experienced. The idea of the book is to learn from my mistakes and make your trips much easier than mine were!

Okay, why did I say don't do it? There are actually many reasons, but the most important are: Because, it will be cold, wet ,and slippery. There will be sand, snow, and ice on the road. In some stage, you will want to quit, but it's not going to be possible. Because of the salty water, your bike might have some electrical problems later. Part of your gear will be damaged from the sand, from the cold, and from the ice.

It sounds a bit discouraging, don't you think? Yes, but I am telling you the truth, exactly how it is!

After so many negative thoughts, let me tell you something more optimistic. Believe it or not, the most difficult part of the trip will be the decision making. Once you have done it, everything will become simple. Yes, it will be cold, tough, and the mileage will be different to usual, but you will be fine, and in the end, you will remember it forever.

After everything I just told you, if you still want to go then keep reading, and I will tell you how to do it!

N: 1 - Prepare the bike carefully.

Keep in mind, that to ride in such conditions is almost the same as to ride off-road. The most important part is to be as light as possible. Do not over pack! Do not take tents, sleeping bag, cooking stoves or any other camping gear. Do not take any additional clothes, shoes or whatever, because you don't need it. After you spend 10 hours riding in the cold, the last thing you will do is to walk around. In fact, all the clothes I have were already worn by my already.

Keep the most important stuff in your pockets or in your tank bag. It is not fun to try to find something in your hard case or saddle bag when the temperature outside is below zero. Keep your hydration pack in the luggage, not on you, because it will freeze. Keep a hat and additional simple gloves in the tank bag. You might need it when you stop and remove your helmet. A big windscreen, hand guards and heated grips are a must. Without them, you can't make it.

Choose the right tires. As I said, to ride in these conditions is about the same as to ride off-road. To have the right tires is critical. I did it with a TKC 80, and I can highly recommend it. You need softer and more aggressive tires. Do not make compromises, because your life depends on it. Just to complete the bike preparation I will repeat again, I really hope that you will remember it!

The weight always matters! Keep the bike as light as possible!

N: 2 - Choose the right clothes

The best, of course, will be to have a heated seat, heated vest, gloves or whatever you can afford, but you can do it even with simple stuff, the one's you already have at home. I did it with the gear that I already had.

Upper body:

T-shirt short sleeves;

T-shirt long sleeves;

Switcher;

Warm lining of the jacket;

Rain gear (top).

Lower body:

Leggings;

Warm lining pants;

Rain gear (pants).

Feet:

Light socks;

Plastic bags (garbage);

Wool socks;

Boots;

Rain covers.

As you can see, there is nothing fancy in my gear. Of course, if you have any heated gloves, vest or any electric gear, it will help, but you can do it even without it if you are just a bit more creative. For example, I used my hydration pack to warm my body. What I did it actually was to refill it with hot water every time when I stopped, and I kept it inside of my jacket. This helped to keep my upper body warm for at least half an hour.

Heated grips are must, you cannot do it without them. The combination between heated grips and the hot hydration pack in my jacket actually warmed the blood around my body which allowed me to ride for at least an hour before I started to feel the cold. The problem after that was that my feet are freezing and I had to stop anyway.

N: 3 - Plan more days.

Riding in such conditions is not like riding in the summer. You will definitely need more time. Plan extra days if the weather gets worse. The last thing you are going to need is to be pressed for time. 300 to 500 km per day is more than enough, even if you have only highways to ride. Keep in mind, that you need to stop almost every hour and every break will take a minimum of 30 minutes from your total time, even if you stop for only 15 minutes, the total time you lose will be 30 minutes. Do not forget to drink enough water when you stop. In winter conditions, the body loses water very quickly. If you notice that you are not going to the toilet on every stop or when you go it's just a few drops of a very dark yellow color, that is a sign of dehydration, and you have to drink more.

N: 4 - Ride slowly.

Sounds easy, but believe me it is not. When you see that the road ahead is clean, you would like to twist the throttle and go faster, but this is not a good idea, because you don't know what it is going to be after. There will be a lot of sand left from the winter, especially on the corners or even worse - black ice. You have to keep yourself calm and expect anything at any moment. I know that is hard to ride with 80km/h when you have to cover 500 or 600km, but this is the right way.

If you have to ride on the snow, then make it even slower. Go to second gear, or first if necessary. Keep the throttle stable and let the tires do the job. Do not use the front brake, especially on the corners! Use the engine brake and the throttle to control the speed and keep the bike as straight as possible. Lose yourself, do not grab the handlebar tight, hold the bike with your knees, not with your hands.

If you have traction control or ABS, I will recommend turning it off, if it's possible. You can turn it on again when you get out of the snow.

N: 5 - Safety first.

Do not push yourself to do the impossible job, just to prove something. Do not try to beat the time or to make some kind of record, because you cannot. For that purpose, we already have the Guinness Book of Records.

Take it easy and ride at your own pace. The most important part is to get back home safe in one piece! Somebody loves you and waits for you at home – never forget that.

To complete what I just said, I will tell you one real story. One guy asked me on my Facebook page about winter tires for a motorcycle. As far I know, these types of tires exist, but they have spikes on it and they are not really for road use. The reason he was asking is that he planned to go from Paris to Norway in January.

Of course, I told him exactly what I said to you – Don't do it! He, of course, said that the decision is taken and he wants to make this great adventure because no one did it before, this would help him to be noticed and many more like this.

I tried, really hard to explain to him the danger of such an adventure and the reason why no one did it is that it is not fun at all and it is very risky. Then he asked me:

'If it's so dangerous, why did you do it?'

I expected the question and told him the truth. I did not expect the weather to change so dramatically. It was almost 10 degrees on the day before and minus 7 on the day I started. It became minus 10 in Prague and even started to snow. The roads were still clean, but a couple of km after that the situation gets really bad. The problem was that I was already 600km away from Berlin. I planned the trip, I moved all my appointments, I had this free window, and it was too late for going back. Long story short, I did somehow, but I will never do it again unless it is absolutely necessary!

Even so, he refused to change his plans and started the trip. A few days later he wrote to me again:

'You were right, I slid on the ice.'

Luckily he was okay. A bent knee, but nothing more serious, but he learned the lesson the hard way. Do not be like him.

*****

High Altitude

If the desired destination you plan to go to includes some high elevation roads, you might be wondering how to prepare yourself. In the following pages, I will share everything I know about it.

In the last few years, I have had the chance to visit some of the high elevation roads, like Zojila pass, India 3,500m (11,575f), Babusar Top, Pakistan 4,173m (13,691f), Ak-Baital pass, Tajikistan, 4,665m, (15,272f), Khunjerab pass, Pakistan 4,880m (16,010f),Taglangla India, 5,328m (17480f) the second highest pass i the world and Khardungla pass, India 5,602m (18,380f) which is known as the highest motorable road in the world.

I believe that the information I can share in this chapter will definitely help you to make your trip much easier and safer.

I will split everything into three simple questions:

N: 1 - How difficult is to ride a motorcycle at high altitude?

Well, the question is simple, but the answer is a bit more complicated. It could be very easy, but it could also be an impossible mission for many. It really depends on your physical and health condition at the moment, and also about the time you are going to give yourself to adapt. Let me explain with more details:

If you try to go there just like that, you will face an impossible task. It doesn't matter how much of a tough guy you are or how many push-ups you can make, this is something completely different. If you never been to such an altitude, your body has no idea of how to react. Yes, it's correct, the body has a memory for everything we do. It is a very clever biological computer and always works for your safety. For example, if you have been to altitude of 3,000m once, the next time it will be much easier than the time before. It's just like anything new in our life.

To have a trouble-free journey you have to make sure that you have enough time to acclimatize. We all understand that and know what we have to do, but sometimes the time is not enough, and we push to the limits believing that we are going to be okay.

I can give you one personal example:

In 2015, we were riding on the Pamir highway in Tajikistan. On one of the days, we spent the night at 2,000m, and after a couple of hours, we climbed to over 4,000m. The riding was fine, I was excited to be there and everything was fine, but once we got to the top and spent a few hours there, the elevation hit me like a wall. With the combination of heavy diarrhea, it became really bad. Simple things, like unloading or loading my motorcycle felt like such heavy work. Most of the time, I was in some kind of delusion mode, and I had this constant headache.

Even today, I don't know if it was from the high altitude, from the food poisoning or from both, but it was hard. The problem was, that we had to spend the entire week at this altitude, even going higher, so I had no chance to become better because the only cure in this situation is to go down. Anyway, it was a hard week and the only moment I was feeling good was when I rode, because I needed to concentrate on the road.

After I learned my lesson in Tajikistan, on my next high elevation trip to Ladakh, I did it the proper way. Thanks to my friend Anurag, who made a great route for me I was able to climb the mountain slowly, step by step, giving enough time to my body to acclimatize and work trouble-free for my entire trip. So, even though I went more than 1,000m higher than I had ever been before, I didn't have any problems. So, the lesson I have learned is to always allow enough time for acclimatization.

N: 2 - Is there any risk?

The simple answer is **YES**, and you have to be very serious when you plan such a trip. This is not a joke, this is not a Sunday ride! To travel at high altitude is already a risk, but there are more than enough unexpected circumstances, and each one of them could put you in serious danger at any given moment. Never underestimate the situation. If you are well prepared and everything goes well, then okay, great; but if something goes wrong, then you have to be ready to react regarding the situation.

Preparation is the key to success. You have already taken the right decision by reading this book, and I am very serious about it. Simple things like a flat tire or any breakdown situation could become a serious problem if you cannot fix it. I already told you the story about my flat tire in Ladakh. Luckily I was able to get out of the situation, but it was a lesson I learned for the future.

Another serious danger is the weather. When you stay down there at 30 degrees, it is hard to believe that at the top, it could be minus 5. Make sure that you have warm clothes because in case of an accident, you might need to spend hours, maybe days there. The weather will be completely different, and even if it's nice and sunny, it could change very fast.

N: 3 - How do you prepare the bike?

There are many discussions about what bike, EFI or carburetor? Many prefer EFI because you don't need to adjust anything and it works well at any altitude… which is partly right, you don't need to touch anything, but even an EFI motorcycle has a lack of power because of the thin air. With EFI Benelli, I was not able to have more than second gear on Babusar top at 4,200m, but with carburetor Himalayan, I was okay even over 5,300m after a simple adjustment of course. In most of the cases, it's a very simple procedure, but you have to know what exactly to do. So, my opinion is that any bike will work fine and you don't even need to worry about it, just ride whatever machine you have.

After all of that being said, I will give you a few simple pieces of advice, and I really hope that you will remember them :

N: 1 - Never go alone. You have to make sure that at least one person knows your location all the time.

N: 2 - Do not even think that you can make it because you are a tough guy. You don't need to learn it the hard way.

N: 3 - Make sure that you have enough time to acclimatize.

N: 4 - Never stay longer than you should. Overnight only if it's an absolute must.

N: 5 - Get the right clothes. The weather at high altitude is different and changes very fast.

N: 6 - Nothing is more important than your life.

Remember this advice and I can guarantee that they will help you to come back safe and in one piece.

*****

What to eat and what to avoid?

I planned to talk about it for a long time, but somehow, I always said later, later… Maybe because I was never really prepared for this direction. I usually have a very detailed strategy for every trip, but the food has never been a part of it. It might sound a bit strange, but I will try to explain what I think about it in this chapter.

I will try to point you in another direction, to show you a different point of view. I want you to see the full picture instead of focusing on the small and not so necessary things. I believe that you hold this book now, because of the different points of view I always offer you, and I have no plans to change it in the near future.

Okay, it is obvious that we need to eat, but what and where? The most popular options are to eat out in restaurants or to cook your food. The first option (eat in restaurants) could be very expensive, especially around Europe or very difficult and even dangerous around Asia for example.

As usual, I will give you a few examples:

In Europe, a meal for one person will cost you between 10 and 30 euro, let's say 15 euro. For a 30-day trip, you will eat at least twice per day which will cost around 900 euro, and I am not talking about fancy restaurants, just basic food, no drinks or stuff like that. It is about the same in the USA, but in dollars. In the UK, Scotland, and Ireland it could be even more; around the Scandinavian countries, this budget will be just for coffee and snacks.

On the other hand, around Asia, the street food can be very cheap. For example, a good meal for one person will cost you 1 or 2 dollars, but the type of food and the variations are limited or at least not so familiar for us. Sometimes, I just don't know what most of the dishes mean or what they have inside.

The language barrier is another problem, you cannot order what you need because they cannot understand you. It is not like Europe where you can expect a large menu in English with nice photos. You can have this, but not everywhere and not every day. All of this makes the simple food choice a very difficult task.

Another serious thing to consider is the products they use. In Central Asia, for example, they cook the food with cotton oil. In Pakistan, India and Nepal, it, was Palm oil and Soya oil in Bangladesh, and many more. They also use different and sometimes too many spices, and the food is just different. In China, for example, the food I ate there has nothing in common with the Chinese food that is found in Europe.

I am not saying that the food in those countries is bad, what I am basically trying to say is that it's different and in most of the cases our stomachs are not ready to take it.

To reply to your question, before you even asked, is that a problem – Ooo yes! In my last trip, I had very bad diahhrea many times. Once in Pakistan, two times in India, once in Nepal and once in Bangladesh.

Basically, every time when I change country, I need to spend at least one day in this condition. The question is not if, it is when? It could be from the food itself or from bad hygiene in those places, but the result is always the same, at least for me.

With all of that being said, you might come to the conclusion that the best option is to cook your own food, but is it really that easy and how much will it cost you? Just to let you know, that I have tried this as well.

Let's see, a good stove will cost you 70-80 dollars. Okay, let's say that you bought a cooking stove. If it's petrol, good, if not, you will need gas. Altogether, it will be around $100.

Now, of course, many of your friends will show you different options for very cheap solutions or brands, but … ask them again after they have used the recommended stuff at least 10 times.

So, stove and fuel – 100 Dollars. You might say – this is not a big deal, I can afford it! Yes, but you cannot cook a meal only with a stove, you will need a number of items, cups, plates, forks, spoons, knives, oil, and spices. Then you will need coffee, tea, sugar… and much more. Before you even notice, the bill will be 500 dollars and at least 2-3 kg in your luggage, which is much worse than the price itself.

Again you might say, it is a good investment and I can use it many times.

Many times? How many exactly? How many times are you going to have the time and will to cook your food? Maybe on the shortstop on the highway, you will open the bags, start the stove and boil water for rice or pasta? Forget about it. You will use it a maximum of once per day or every couple of days only.

If you are out wild camping, you will need to wash everything in the river, which is not so easy if you don't have the proper cleaning materials. In the camping spots, they usually have a kitchen and stoves, so you don't really need yours.

I would say that if you are an average person, like 90% of the travelers I met in the last 10 years you will cook your food once per three or four days. Usually in the camping kitchen or in the hostel. Also, have you ever tried to cook something? It is not that easy. Especially when you don't have the proper space, necessary dishes, plates, knives, and many more.

Again, you might resist and say that there are many options of prefabricated meals, and all you need is just to boil water. Yes, that is true, but the ones you can buy very cheaply are crap and the good, so-called mountain food, or any other high-calorie packs usually cost between 8 and 15 dollars for one person, and how many of these you can carry with you – 30?

I have seen many of my riding friends buying all these. They carry useless kitchen stuff and tons of food and never use it. I did it before as well. I have everything at home, and in the last few trips, I did not even take it with me.

I know that it might look cool on pictures, but it is definitely not what you expect, and you are not going to do it as often you might think, but you will definitely carry all the weight with you. 3 kg here, 5 kg there and in the end, you will finish with 70kg of luggage. Anyway, the chapter is about the food not about the weight, let's go back to the topic.

What is the solution, what can you do? What can you eat? Because it is obvious that we need to eat.

Well…I am glad that you expect me to tell you that, but I cannot. Everybody prefers something different. One person will be happy to stop at every fancy restaurant another will try to save money and will eat only fast food. Like anything else, it is very subjective and it depends on you.

What I will do is to tell you the simple truth. I want to prepare you for everything that is about to come, not because I am very clever, it is because I have already been there. As I said, I already tried all the options and finished with something completely different, and it worked, for me perfectly in the last couple of years. So, before I tell you the answers, I have some questions for you:

- What is the most important part of your trip?
- Do you travel because you love it or do you have another reason?
- Are ready to step out of your comfort zone?
- Do you plan to travel or to cook three times per day?
- Are you ready to answer these questions honestly?

What I do, is to search for food when I need to. Any supermarket or similar will be okay. They usually have many products, and at least a few of these will be well known, and I can eat it without even worrying about it. In the worse scenario, they will have biscuits or some dry food.

Later in the evening when I find a place to sleep, I can have a nice dinner or something different. The food has never been something so critical for me. In most of my long riding days, I survived on biscuits and tea. Especially when I am fighting with the time to sit somewhere and spend 1 hour for lunch, it's nonsense for me.

If I have to go to a remote area without any chances to get food, I will just buy something before that, it is so simple.

I know that this might catch you unprepared, but this was the idea. Focus on the trip, not on the food. Don't even think about it, the food you can find everywhere around the world. Even in the most remote areas, people still need to eat. It might not be what you prefer or it might taste a bit different, but so what? Everything is part of the adventure!

A man could survive 30 days without food, but only a couple of days without water.

Everybody is buying camping adventure stuff, but not many of you use a hydration pack for example. Which is much more important if you ask me.

*****

How to stay hydrated?

It's always amazed me how something so important is so underestimated! Most of you will spend so much time and energy on different adventure gadgets, but will ever think of just how important it is to stay hydrated. A hydration pack costs virtually nothing compared to the rest of the gear, but it is a must-have item for every long distance motorcycle rider.

I don't know how many travelers I have met on the road in the last 10 years, but I have to say that only about 20% had hydration packs.

I don't know why, but people always underestimate the need of such an item.

On the long riding days, I will recommend drinking water all the time. When you are thirsty, it is already too late. Even if you are not thirsty, you have to drink. When you don't have enough water, you start to lose concentration and the best way to fix it is by having a hydration pack.

You can drink once every 15 minutes, half an hour or more. You can have just a couple of drops, but it will keep you concentrating at all times.

Most of you believe that it is the same if you just have a simple bottle of water. Before I continue, I want to tell you about an example from my last trip.

In Pakistan, my riding friend Anif didn't have a hydration pack. He has a bottle of water, but it stays in his hard case. That means that every time when he decided to drink, we needed to stop, remove the helmet, the gloves, open his hard case and drink.

Do you think that he did it all the time? No, even though it was so hot. He also had a mesh jacket that even helped him to dehydrate his body even faster. So, on one of our stops I saw that he was a bit nervous, his hands were shaking, and his reactions were different. I asked him how many times he had drank water and he said just once. Once! It was two in the afternoon, and I finished two litters already! He just didn't want to stop.

Another example, is when you fight with the time, ride in the rain or on a busy road with a lot of trucks, you just overtake them all and now, if you stop, you have to do it again and many more. When it has happened, you will simply ignore the water until the next stop. This is exactly what Anif did. In most cases, this will be fine, but there will be some moments when this will be a very bad idea.

When we were in Central Asia with Dima, on some of the days we hit temperatures of over 46 degrees. For more than a week, we had to drink more than 10l of water per day and we never went to the toilet. We actually started to use the toilet normally when we went to Pamir Mountain. I had my hydration pack, but Dima didn't. Luckily, he managed to get through without any serious problems, but we needed to stop many times, all because he need to drink or because he dropped the bottle, forgot to close the cap or burned on the exhausts. Since then, he always carries a hydration pack

Another benefit of having it is that it is always there in my backpack and I use it all the time. It doesn't matter where I am, on the bike or around the city. If you have a bottle, you need to hold it. Even when I go to bed or in the tent, I always take it with me.

The only moment where I could not use it was last winter on my trip to the Balkans, this was only because it was too cold. Actually, the weather forced me to stop more often, so I was able to drink enough and stay hydrated.

You have to know that when you travel with a motorcycle, your body consumes double, maybe triple the amount of water and this is when the conditions are normal. When the temperature rises above 35 degrees, it becomes a totally different story. Especially if you do it with a mesh jacket or even worse, you ride with a t-shirt and sandals. You will be actually drying like a fish under the sun.

Another example is on the very cold days. When you ride in the cold weather, the body needs double the amount of normal water, that's why hikers need to melt snow. Also, when you travel at a high elevation, just as I did in India, you need to drink much more than you normally do. So water really is everything!

As I told you in the previous chapter, a man could survive without food for one month, but only a couple of days or even hours depending on the conditions without water. If this is not a reason to have it, then I don't know what would be!

So, for me, this is one of the most important items after the helmet and my riding gear, and I really hope that you will buy one before your next trip.

*****

You made it!

So, my friend, you have now made it to the end of this book. I hope that by now, you feel complete with all of the information you would ever need to know before you go on the next level of adventures.

I hope you have enjoyed my stories and more importantly, that you have found the information relevant and useful. Now, I will leave to you to get started on planning your next adventure trip!

If you like the book, and of course if you wish, please write a review and send it to my e-mail: zhelev.p@abv.bg, or write it directly on the Amazon system. If you read the e-book version, you can go straight to Amazon review section

I really would like to hear from you. Just to let you know that I also offer a 100% money-back guarantee! If you are not 100% satisfied with your order, I will do everything I can to make it right. But if I can't - I will return your money.

Do not forget to visit my Youtube channel and subscribe to see a new video every week!

I wish you all the best and ask you to always ride safe!

Pavlin Zhelev

www.rtw-adventures.com

Printed in Great Britain
by Amazon